101
ONE HUNDRED AND ONE

Activities for
Social &
Emotional
Resilience

101 Activities & Ideas

Sue Jennings

101 Activities for Empathy & Awareness
101 Ideas for Managing Challenging Behaviour
101 Activities for Social & Emotional Resilience
101 Activities for Increasing Focus & Motivation
101 Activities for Positive Thoughts & Feelings

101
ONE HUNDRED AND ONE

Activities for Social & Emotional Resilience

Sue Jennings

HINTON HOUSE Emotional Literacy Resources

HINTONHOUSE

Dedication

This book is dedicated to my wonderful team,
dramatherapist Penny Mcfarlane and play therapist
Ali Chown, who are both such creative people.

Illustrations by Matyas Fazakas

First published by

Hinton House Publishers Ltd,

Newman House, 4 High Street, Buckingham, MK18 1NT, UK

T +44 (0)1280 822557   F +44 (0)560 313 5274
E info@hintonpublishers.co.uk

www.hintonpublishers.co.uk

© Sue Jennings, 2013

Printed in the United Kingdom by Hobbs the Printers Ltd

British Library Cataloguing in Publication Data

A CIP catalogue record for this book is available from the British Library.

ISBN 978 1 906531 46 1

FSC
www.fsc.org
MIX
Paper from
responsible sources
FSC® C020438

Contents

Contents

Contents

Contents

About the Author

Sue Jennings PhD is Visiting Professor at Anglia Ruskin University and an Honorary Fellow at Leeds Metropolitan University. She has been a pioneering influence in the development of dramatherapy in several countries and has established neuro-dramatic play as an approach to attachment that emphasises the importance of early playfulness. She has written many books, a number of which have been translated into Greek, Korean, Russian, Swedish, Danish and Italian. Her doctoral research was carried out with the Temiar people in the Malaysian rain forest, where she lived with her three children. Currently she trains carers in 'Creative Care', for use in their work with older people and people with dementia. She was awarded a Churchill Fellowship for Arts and Older People in 2012/2013.

www.suejennings.com, www.creativecareinternational.org

Acknowledgments

This book has been inspired by several resilient people with whom I have shared ideas: Steve Mitchell, John Casson, Priscilla Ho, Ditty Doctor and Fraser Brown.

My colleagues in Romania have always supported my research and development: Ioana Serb, Oana Roxana, Jenelle Mazaris, Matyas Fazakas, and many creative and risk-taking students.

Sarah Miles, as always, is a very supportive publisher and gives me lots of freedom!

Sue Jennings
Stratford-upon-Avon
2013

Introduction

What is Resilience?

Resilience is the capacity to manage the ups and down of life without being overwhelmed by unexpected events such as accidents or loss. Children learn resilience through healthy attachments within their families and with parents who acknowledge a child's fears and anxieties, rather than dismissing them with 'don't be silly, there are no ghosts' (or monsters under the bed, or snakes in the wardrobe). Resilient children are able to manage stresses in their lives, especially if they live in stable and supportive families where there is trust and nurture. These include adults who will listen to fears and anxieties and help children express and understand them.

Much is being written about resilience and how it can develop in some children despite traumatic experiences. Children respond to different crises in significantly different ways and the younger the child the more vulnerable they are to stress reaction (Jennings, 2011). Children can become traumatised if they cannot grasp the meaning of an event.

According to Garmezy and Rutter (1983), 'Children are more resilient if they are born with easy temperaments and are in good mental health. If they are lucky enough to have strong parents who can withstand the stresses of poverty and community violence, children have a better chance of growing into happy and productive adults.'

Marston (2001) has identified resilience in those children and young adults 'who have the capacity to "hold onto meaning", to give the events in their lives an emotional framework that somehow lets them cope more effectively.' She asks, 'what is the "ordinary magic"?', by which she means those factors that provide at least part of what is needed to help children survive acute life events and move on to healthy adulthood.

Cyrulnik (2005), in a major contribution to our understanding of trauma and resilience, suggests that there are two main features of the resilient child: bond and meaning. However, he suggests that resilience is not a recipe for happiness; rather it is 'a strategy for struggle against unhappiness, that makes it possible to seize some pleasure in life despite the whispering of ghosts in the depths of our memory'. His book, *The Whispering of Ghosts: Trauma and Resilience*, discusses the traumatic lives of Marilyn Monroe and Hans Christian Anderson, and how they survived humiliation, loss and degradation during childhood. They reached adulthood at great cost to themselves, Marilyn to be exploited both financially and sexually, and Hans to create the most wonderful fairy stories although he was unable to find intimacy with women in his personal life.

It is estimated that 80 per cent of all children exposed to powerful stressors do not manifest developmental damage (Rutter, 1979; Werner, 1990). There are certain factors that contribute to this resilience: the child's physical and social environment; a stable, emotional relationship with at least one parent or another significant adult; and a supportive educational environment. Parents act as an emotional 'buffer' for the child who is developing strength and resilience. According to Garbarino *et al* (1992), 'Most children are able to cope with dangerous environments and maintain resilience as long as their parents are not stressed beyond their capacity to cope.'

It is of vital importance that teachers and others who work with children are given the knowledge and skills to address issues of resilience. It is possible to develop greater resilience in both children and teenagers when it is clear they are unable to cope with adversity. This inability to cope may result from their early parenting, disruption of their home life, or numerous foster placements; in general, the lack of an environment where they have been able to establish a caring and trusting relationship. Loss of resilience may also occur where there is a lack of coping with a traumatic incident such as a train or plane crash, sudden death or other major shock. Parents themselves may be overwhelmed by the incident, or may not have survived and are therefore unavailable to support the child or teenager.

Erikson (1965) maintains that learning to trust is the most important task for the infant. Learning 'Basic Trust versus Mistrust' is the first of Erikson's eight stages of social and emotional development. It occurs during the first two years and is based on the way a child is cared for and loved; whether he or she has formed a 'secure attachment'. Trust and security allow resilience and optimism to develop. If trust does not develop, a child will be insecure, mistrustful and often scared of life.

Children who have not learned to trust through their primary attachment relationship will often have difficulties in their social relationships in later life. The more secure the child, the more resilient they become, and the more able to manage adversity and difficulties as they grow up.

Managing Fears

If we dismiss children's fears and expect them to 'toughen up', we are embarking on a self-defeating strategy. McCarthey (2007, p. 19) addresses this succinctly in his exceptional book *If You Turned into a Monster*, in which he says:

> Monsters are after all our first creative acts as humans. From early on we dream them and imagine them. They dwell under our beds or behind our bedroom doors. They peek in through our windows. They are often right at the edge of our developing consciousness, part instinctual urge and part deity. We wake our parents in the middle of the night because of them, and our parents try ineffectually to dispel them by saying things like 'There's no such thing as monsters' or 'It was just a dream'.

Monsters are just one way of giving form to feeling and the feeling is very real. Basic fear lies behind most difficult behaviour, including anger and violence. And, of course, lack of resilience. The resilient child or teenager is able to trust themselves and other people, and to deal with adversity with the support of a coping adult where appropriate.

The techniques in this book are carefully structured in order to allow for the development of resilience strengths in children and young people. The creative methods chosen have been proved to be effective with all age groups and do not demand extensive previous training. Indeed, use of the book could itself be regarded as training, since clear guidelines for the process are given throughout.

One of my inspirations for this book has been the words of Nelson Mandela: 'Let bygones be bygones.' After all that he had suffered, he was still able to maintain his resilience and let go of the whispering ghosts.

The Philosophy of this Book

I am very motivated by the concepts of Positive Psychology (Grenville-Cleave, 2012), in which it is important to focus on what people *can* do. Too often the experience of children and teenagers is a dismal one that only reinforces what they *cannot* do. This can become a vicious cycle between home and school, and the individual ends up feeling demoralised. I also think that the growth of 'mindfulness' (Williams & Penman, 2011) is useful in our work, as it helps to keep even the most desperate group leader a little more positive.

Neuroscience currently has a big influence in education and therapy, and there is a greater understanding of how early experiences help to shape thought processes. Bodies and brains influence each other and we no longer recognise the 'nature–nurture' split (Jennings, 2011).

How to Use this Book

Aims

Discuss the aims of the whole series of activities with the group, and repeat these each week if necessary. They are: to build up confidence, deal with worries, check out concerns regarding bullying, develop stronger friendships, find ways to communicate in families, and to develop coping skills in daily life.

Confidentiality

It is very important to establish a confidentiality rule, because this encourages people to share their experiences. It is also a good way of developing trust within a group.

Disclosures

It is not uncommon in an experiential group for an individual to disclose traumatic experiences such as sexual abuse, physical assault, bullying and emotional tyranny. It is important that your school or group safeguarding policy is followed and the appropriate authorities are notified.

Bullying & Intimidation

If something of this nature is happening within the school, it is essential that the school's anti-bullying policy is enforced. This is in addition to the various exercises that address bullying.

Terminology

De-roling

At the end of an exercise or a session it is important to come out of the role or character that has been played. Individuals can literally shake off a character, or say their own name very loudly, or play a quick energy game. Everyone needs to 'inhabit themselves' again before leaving the session.

Freeze

This is a command for everyone to stand still, without changing their position, prior to receiving a new instruction. Freeze can be practised as part of a warm-up so that participants are clear that the command is fundamental to the group's work and must be obeyed.

Freeze-frame (or sculpting)

The group members freeze to make a picture. This is used as a way to tell a story; it brings the action to life but is not as frightening as enactment can be for some people. It is usually used in threes, with a freeze-frame each for the beginning, middle and end of the story.

Tableau

This tells the whole story in the same way as the freeze-frame, but the tableau is like a single snapshot of an event and can use all of the group members, in role, in the picture.

WGC/ICh

Whole Group Consultation, Individual Choice. During later warm-ups the group members choose what they want to do. After group discussion a leader is chosen to select and lead the warm-up.

General guidelines for activities

Use of voice to guide a session

Try to be firm, relaxed, calm, soothing and make use of positive indicators, such as affirming individuals when they manage small steps.

Use 'feeling' words

It is important to make use of feeling words as much as possible when discussing themes and issues. The words are not related directly to the group members, but can acknowledge your own feelings at being late, or frustrated when the car doesn't start, or being pleased when it doesn't rain. Most young people lack the language and concepts to acknowledge how they are feeling. By using the 'feeling' words ourselves we are role-modelling and learning together.

Workbooks & folders

Have available a workbook and a folder for each group member. Most activities suggest drawing or writing in workbooks as an ending. Folders can be used to store worksheets and keep safe artwork created during activities.

Fleeces

Having a fleece blanket for each person is a great way of relaxing at the end of a session.

Drum

The use of a drum is very important to attract people's attention and to indicate the start and finish of an exercise. It is also used for rhythmic exercises with people who are 'out of rhythm'. Drumming as a group, if resources permit, is a very good way of building group cohesion and focusing energy.

Warm-ups

During a warm-up the participants in a group are able to let go of physical tension, ignore distractions and focus on the task in hand. Most warm-ups in this book have three stages:

1 The invitation to join the group and sit in the welcoming circle. This is a time for acknowledgement and learning names.

2 The aims of the session are then stated clearly, allowing time for questions, followed by an introduction of the themes: group members are encouraged to throw ideas around and these are written on the board. The aims need to be transparent.

3 The third stage is one of physical activity, during which games, drama exercises and stop–start techniques are developed. Warm-ups are suggested for the early activities but, as participants become more confident, they can negotiate within the group to choose a warm-up themselves.

Warm-up Ideas

1 'Tag' and 'chain tag', and other playground games.

2 Hold hands in big circle and struggle, without breaking the circle.

3 'Touch four corners of the room, jump up and down three times, and shout your name loudly and then softly – in one minute!'

4 'Stretch and bend, follow a friend, call a greeting, enjoy the meeting!'

5 Travel across the room as if on skates.

6 Travel across the room as if wearing giant's boots.

7 Travel across the room on hands and feet.

8 Pretend you are holding a large, strong balloon and keep it in the air.

9 Pretend you are holding a large, strong balloon and pat it to and fro as you cross the room.

10 Newspaper islands: take a number of pieces of newspaper, one less than the number of people in the group. Scatter the pieces around the room and, when the drum beats, each person stands on some newspaper; one person will be 'out'. Remove one piece of newspaper in each round until there is only one person left.

11 As above, but halve the number of newspapers; when the drum beats everyone stands on a piece of newspaper with a partner.

12 Stretch up and imagine you are picking cherries from a tree.

13 Stretch up and imagine you are pulling stars from the sky.

14 In threes, discover the least number of body parts you can allow to touch the floor without falling over.

15 Bounce a ball to a partner without losing continuity; then repeat.

16 In twos, hold your partner with both hands and pull them across the space; the partner being pulled places their feet firmly on the ground to resist.

17 Scatter around the room, then freeze; scatter again, then freeze.

18 With a partner, talk in a made-up language for one minute.

19 With a partner, talk in numbers instead of words for one minute.

20 With a partner, ask a question; the partner answers a completely different question.

Part One
Dealing with Feelings: Trapped in the Web

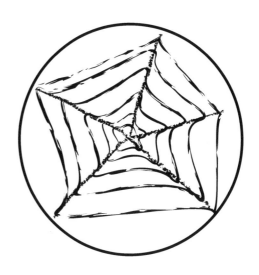

Activities

Worksheets

Story Sheet

Introduction

Many children and young people have become trapped in a destructive cycle of behaviour and emotions. They have lost the capacity for resilience, or have not been able to achieve it, and therefore lack a brain 'executive function' for managing the ups and down of life. Often they lack concentration and are easily distracted, or become preoccupied with their own anxieties and worries. They may feel 'all over the place' or lost, or otherwise try to hold themselves together with tension and preoccupation.

The techniques in this section address these particular issues and serve as an introduction to this approach to developing resilience. It may be that some groups need further preparatory work before embarking on the following section. It can be useful to address two main issues. The first is physical containment, this can be addressed through warm-up techniques (see Introduction), ball exercises, basic running and jumping, stop-start-freeze. Many participants need to find 'easy-to-manage' space for their bodies. The second issue is the individual who feels unable to 'take a first step' or 'make a first mark'. They are so contained and self-absorbed that they feel fearful of making a commitment to explore. Warm-up games would be anxiety provoking, whereas a quiet relaxation exercise could be helpful. For example, inviting the group to look at the floor or the ceiling (closing eyes can increase anxiety), to listen to their own breathing, and to think about a nice place.

It is important to work at the pace of the group, always remembering to support what they can do, rather than unwittingly creating another failure situation.

1 Feeling Free

 Children Teenagers

> **Aims** To encourage participants to develop security in the group and to feel free to express any worries.

> **Materials** Large whiteboard, coloured markers, fleeces, mats, large drum(s), personal folders and workbooks, crayons and coloured pens; Worksheets 1 and 2.

Warm Up Invite everyone to sit in the group and learn each other's names and the name each person likes to be known by. If the group is from the same class or already know each other, encourage them to discuss their names.

Discuss the aims of the whole series of activities: to build up confidence, deal with any worries, check out concerns regarding bullying, develop stronger friendships, and to find ways to communicate in families. Write key words on the board. Worksheet 1 'Group Contract and Agreement', can be used to clarify the aims and rules of the group.

The aim for this session is an active 'getting to know you', in order to decrease stress. Everyone scatters around the room and 'freezes'. Invite everyone to stretch out, as far as they can, their arms and legs, without actually touching anyone else, then slowly to crouch down to make themselves as small as possible. Scatter again and freeze; slowly grow as tall as possible and 'walk tall' around the room; repeat and now 'walk tall' with a partner.

Activities Suggest to group members that they are stuck in a giant spider's web, or some other kind of alien environment:

- ✪ Practise being really 'stuck' and not able to move.
- ✪ Feel the web binding closer and closer so that it slowly wraps arms against bodies and feet tightly together.
- ✪ Move awkwardly to someone else.
- ✪ If two people can touch hands they can free each other.
- ✪ Colour and write on Worksheet 2, 'I Feel Trapped'.

> **Sharing** Talk about how it feels to be stuck and then released.

> **Closure** Draw a web in workbooks and relax with fleeces.

Dealing with Feelings: Trapped in the Web

2 Feeling Tense

 Children  Teenagers

> **Aims** For participants to identify where they feel stressed and practise relaxation.

> **Materials** Large whiteboard, coloured markers, fleeces, mats, large drum(s), personal folders and workbooks, crayons and coloured pens; Worksheet 3.

Warm Up Invite everyone into the circle and check for feedback from the previous session. Explain that this session is for de-stressing the body. Give examples, such as, 'Many people have aches in their shoulders, or stomachs, headaches, and so on ...' Invite people to use Worksheet 3, 'Where Do I Feel Hurt?', to describe where they feel tense. They can also use the whiteboard: each person calls out an area of the body that feels tense, then writes it or colours it in on the board.

 If anyone shows a worrying level of stress or aches, seek advice. For example, some participants may be bruised from bullying or being beaten, or from self-harm.

Walk around the room; run around the room; run in and out between the others in the room without touching anyone; use a drum if necessary.

Activities Everyone lies on an individual mat with a fleece and their workbook at their side:
- ✪ Stretch the whole body (suggest that younger children stretch like a starfish), then relax.
- ✪ Stretch the whole body, then curl up, then relax.
- ✪ Draw both knees up, and then relax.
- ✪ Stretch both arms up and relax, clench both fists and relax.
- ✪ Everyone rolls onto their side and curls up to relax.
- ✪ Repeat the sequence even more slowly.

> **Sharing** Turn to someone nearby and help them slowly to sit up.

> **Closure** Write one word about relaxation in workbooks; relax with fleeces.

Dealing with Feelings: Trapped in the Web

3 Ignoring Distractions

 Children   Teenagers

Aims To develop concentration and decrease distraction.

Materials Large whiteboard, coloured markers, fleeces, mats, large drum(s), personal folders and workbooks, crayons and coloured pens.

Warm Up Invite everyone into the circle and check for any feedback from the previous session. Explain that this session is about increasing concentration and decreasing distraction: write on the board key words for things that group members find distracting, such as the sound of a chair scraping, roadworks (external sounds), and so on.

Everyone has a body-stretch and shakes out arms, hands, legs, one at a time. Explain that everyone is going to walk in straight lines in the room, turning at the corners and continuing to walk. Meanwhile, call out directions to try and distract, such as 'over here', 'run and jump', 'faster', and so on. 'Freeze' is when everyone stops; finish with a repeat of the shake-out.

Activities The following mental exercise is to assist concentration and focus; participants may choose to sit back-to-back in twos or threes:

- ✪ Close or shade the eyes and think about trees, any sort of a tree.
- ✪ Imagine one tree with leaves or spines when it is beginning to grow.
- ✪ Imagine it is growing in size and producing blossoms or fruit or cones.
- ✪ Now concentrate very hard on the detail of the tree.
- ✪ Slowly open eyes and draw your tree in the your workbook.

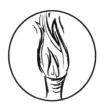

This exercise uses a specific 'graded focus': participants focus on trees generally; then choose one individual tree; then concentrate on its growth and change; and then they recreate it in their workbooks. This approach channels mental energy into greater awareness of detail.

Sharing Share tree pictures in twos/threes, look at their similarities and differences.

Closure Write or draw in workbooks anything that was distracting; relax with fleeces.

4 Concentration and Focus

 Children   Teenagers

Aims To continue to develop concentration and to understand intrusive thought.

Materials Large whiteboard, coloured markers, fleeces, mats, large drum(s), personal folders and workbooks, crayons and coloured pens.

Warm Up Invite everyone into the circle and check for any feedback from previous session. Explain that this session is a development of last week and includes things that distract us from inside. Give examples, such as: 'I find it hard to concentrate when I realise I have left my car keys somewhere'; or 'My friend is in hospital and I am worried'. Invite suggestions that are not personalised (it is too early for that): ask the group to think about the *type* of thing that could distract someone and write the suggestions on the board. Everyone discharges energy by running around the room and leaping as high as they can!

Activities Invite everyone into a circle and explain the 'demand game', in which someone demands something that can be either realistic or crazy! For example: 'I am your sister, where is my hair-gel?; or 'I am an elephant, where is my trunk?'

- ✪ Go around the circle and everyone asks a demand question of the person next to them – the person listens but does not answer.

- ✪ Go around again and repeat the question and this time the person gives an answer: sensible for a sensible question and silly for a silly question.

- ✪ Repeat with the opposite: silly answer for sensible question and vice versa.

- ✪ Divide the group in half and each group has to decide on a sensible question to ask the other half, which they shout out in unison; each group then shouts out an answer.

- ✪ Each group decides on a silly question to ask the other group, which has to give a silly answer when they are asked the question.

 This exercise may feel just silly! However, it is habituating participants to externalising demanding questions, and allows them the opportunity to 'play' with ideas and concepts. In addition, questions and answers will have to be negotiated in the small group and participants are learning to work together.

Sharing Share in the whole group any feedback about the exercise.

Closure Draw a silly question in workbooks; relax with fleeces.

5 Letting a Worry Go

☑ Children   ☑ Teenagers

Aims To find ways to let go of tension and worries.

Materials Large whiteboard, coloured markers, fleeces, mats, large drum(s), personal folders and workbooks, crayons and coloured pens.

Warm Up Invite everyone into the circle and check for any feedback from previous session. Explain that this session is a combination of letting go of physical tension and pretending to drop worries into a flowing river, which carries them to the sea. Everyone moves into a space and weaves in and out of everyone else without touching their neighbours; suggest that everyone can start by moving with just a small amount of energy, so they are only just moving, and then begin to move more quickly, like a fast-flowing river.

Activities The following exercise will help people to let go of tension and can be varied according to age. When everyone is sitting down, invite them to close their eyes:

- ✪ Imagine it is bread-making time: mix flour and water, which sticks to the fingers so you have to rub your hands together to get rid of it.
- ✪ Mix the dough and kneed with the knuckles, slap it flat and mix again.
- ✪ Roll it and make circles and different shapes.
- ✪ Mould it again while thinking of a worry and shape the worry in the dough.
- ✪ Imagine a river is nearby and, with a big movement, the dough is thrown into the fast-flowing water.
- ✪ Everyone slowly opens their eyes.

Sharing Discuss in the whole group how it felt to physically throw away a worry.

Closure Draw a gently flowing river in workbooks; relax with fleeces.

Dealing with Feelings: Trapped in the Web

6 Where am I? (1)

 Children   Teenagers

Aims	To encourage participants to explore feeling lost and being able to change.

Materials	Large whiteboard, coloured markers, fleeces, mats, large drum(s), personal folders and workbooks, crayons and coloured pens.

Warm Up   Invite everyone into the circle and check for any feedback from previous session. Encourage sharing of emotions about feeling lost and suggest that there are several ways to explore the topic, including a physical approach. Everyone shakes out any tension, then takes a deep breath and shouts out any sound they want. Stand in a space and feel blown by a strong wind, first in one direction and then another.

Activities   Explain that the activities continue from the warm-up and that there will be individual work and group work:

- ⊗ Stay rooted to the spot and, no matter what imaginary forces are pulling and pushing, stay rooted!
- ⊗ With a partner lightly pushing on your shoulder, stay firm as the partner pushes you from either side.
- ⊗ The partner increases the pressure and tests your balance.
- ⊗ Change around and repeat the exercise.
- ⊗ Explore, with a partner, crossing a new land with obstacles and dangers.

Sharing	Discuss in the whole group how easy or difficult it is to find where one is going.

Closure	In workbooks, draw a symbol that says 'me' and colour it; relax with fleeces.

7 Where am I? (2)

✓ Children ✓ Teenagers

Aims To facilitate participants' understanding of how changes can cause tensions and feelings of being lost.

Materials Large whiteboard, coloured markers, fleeces, mats, large drum(s), personal folders and workbooks, crayons and coloured pens; Worksheet 4.

Warm Up Invite everyone into the circle and check for feedback from previous session. Acknowledge different ways in which people can feel lost, such as when they lose maps or directions. Share ideas from the group and write them on the board. Repeat the physical exercise from previous session: shake out any tension; take a deep breath and shout out any sounds that come to mind; and stand in a space and feel blown by a strong wind in one direction and then another.

Activities Everyone works individually using Worksheet 4, 'I Feel Lost', and coloured pens. Answer any questions and remind people of the confidentiality rule.

- ✪ Colour the tree and branches.
- ✪ Look at all the leaves and decide where you are now.
- ✪ Colour the leaf person who is wearing the expression that describes where you are now.
- ✪ Decide where you would like to be.
- ✪ Write or draw underneath a possible change for the picture.

Sharing Suggest a group discussion about the possible changes everyone has drawn on their tree.

Closure Write or draw a positive feeling in workbooks; relax with fleeces.

Dealing with Feelings: Trapped in the Web

8 Knitting Myself Back Together Again

 Children   ✓ Teenagers

Aims To find ways of 'putting yourself together' (rather than '*pulling* yourself together').

Materials Large whiteboard, coloured markers, fleeces, mats, large drum(s), personal folders and workbooks, crayons and coloured pens; Worksheet 5.

Warm Up Invite everyone into the circle and check for any feedback from previous session. Explain that often people feel torn apart or 'unravelled', especially by the unexpected actions of others. However, it is possible to put yourself back together again and therefore take control. First move one arm and shake it, then another limb, and work through several body parts as if they were separate. Then move everything together in a mock sport or dance.

Activities Suggest to group members that sometimes it is hard to heal splits within ourselves, and allow things to be 'sewn up'. Everyone makes groups of three.

- ✪ Two people hold hands and a third person has to try and get between them – roughness not allowed. Everyone takes a turn at being the person who gets between the other two.
- ✪ Repeat this, but with one person in the middle and the other two trying to stop them from breaking out. Everyone has a turn at trying to break out.
- ✪ The groups of three sit back to back and relax; introduce the idea that life can be like a piece of knitting that comes unravelled sometimes.
- ✪ Give Worksheet 5, 'Knitting Myself Back Together', to everyone to colour and fill in.
- ✪ Suggest that the knitting can be continued.

Sharing Share colourings in whole group.

Closure Write or draw a hole that is filled in with colour; relax with fleeces.

9 Finding a Balance

 Children   Teenagers

Aims To explore the balance between feeling trapped and feeling lost.

Materials Large whiteboard, coloured markers, fleeces, mats, large drum(s), personal folders and workbooks, crayons and coloured pens; previous drawings, from personal folders, of being trapped in the web (Worksheet 2) and feeling lost (Worksheet 4).

Warm Up Invite everyone into the circle and check for any feedback from last session. Remind group members of the previous themes of feeling trapped and feeling lost, and explain that today's session will look at the balance between the two. Invite comments and write key words on the whiteboard. Create a physical warm-up during which half the group curl up being trapped and the other half wander around feeling lost; then change around. Stretch the body as high and as wide as possible, then curl up as if in a small box, then stretch very high again.

Activities Invite everyone to look at Worksheets 2 and 4 from their folders and note the differences.

- ✪ Make two groups; one group creates an alien web with a voice.
- ✪ The other group design an anti-web potion.
- ✪ Practise a situation in which group members can capture others by touching their feet.
- ✪ Expand the game so that it fills up the whole room.
- ✪ Suggest the groups find a way to change the web that traps into a shelter that protects; the anti-web potion can become a friendship potion.

Sharing Discuss in the whole group the theme of balance between the two extremes and relate the discussion to everyday life.

Closure Draw a pair of weighing scales in workbooks; relax with fleeces.

10 The Story of the Worry Tree

 Children  Teenagers

Aims	To encourage the externalisation of anxieties and worries.

Materials	Large whiteboard, coloured markers, fleeces, mats, large drum(s), personal folders and workbooks, crayons and coloured pens; Story Sheet 1.

Warm Up Invite everyone into the circle and check for any feedback from previous session. Explain that this session is about getting rid of worries that burden and encouraging the sharing of worries when necessary. Divide the big group into small groups of three or four. In each group one person is running away, while the remainder join hands and pretend to be the 'worry wasps', pursuing and trying to catch the runner. Repeat so everyone has a chance to be a runner.

Activities Read Story Sheet 1, 'The Story of the Worry Tree', while everyone is sitting back to back in twos or threes:

- ✪ Invite everyone to think about a worry tree.
- ✪ How old is it and what shape?
- ✪ Draw and colour the tree in workbooks.
- ✪ Decide how to hang worries on the tree.
- ✪ Draw on the tree three or four packets, bundles or messages containing worries.

Sharing	Discuss in the small groups one worry that is common to children (or teenagers) and ways to solve it.

Closure	In workbooks, draw a bird that might fly away with the worries; relax with fleeces.

Part Two
Dealing with Relationships: Testing & Trusting

Activities

Worksheets

Story Sheet

Introduction

This section is directly related to the previous one and some of the exercises can be combined if appropriate. A recurring theme in resilience is developing the capacity to trust, and many children and young people who feel they are outsiders also admit that they do not trust people. As we know (see Introduction), the capacity to trust develops very early in a child's life, usually between birth and eighteen months. Some children are never able to develop a trusting relationship because of early neglect or lack of parental availability. Others lose their trust following major loss or trauma. However, if there is trauma in the child's life, providing one parent is able to manage the effects, the child will not lose their resilience. Coping parents enable coping children.

The techniques in this section address issues of trusting others and acknowledging feelings about being an outsider. Participants are able to explore these themes without making personal disclosures, through metaphors of nursery rhymes, story characters and by using sculpting and freeze-frames (see Introduction), as well as worksheets.

11 Feeling Good about Myself

 Children   Teenagers

> **Aims** To strengthen self-esteem for children and teenagers who feel burdened by worries, especially about relationships.

> **Materials** Large whiteboard, coloured markers, fleeces, mats, large drum(s), personal folders and workbooks, crayons and coloured pens; Worksheet 6.

Warm Up Invite everyone into the circle and share feedback from previous sessions. Encourage people to share things that make them feel good about themselves and how hard it is to remember these when life gets tough. Write important words and phrases on the board. Invite the group to choose their favourite warm-up game and two people to lead it.

Activities Suggest that people work in pairs and think of a gift they would really like to receive; it could be an actual prize or present, or perhaps something someone could say to them (such as appreciation for helping).

- ✪ Discuss with your partner what you would really like to have – and from whom?
- ✪ Is it a dream or could it happen?
- ✪ What is the nearest gift that is probable?
- ✪ What difference would it make to how you feel?
- ✪ Colour in the rainbow scarf picture on Worksheet 6.

> **Sharing** In the whole group, each person allows their partner to present them with their scarf, with the partner giving a reason for their 'gift'.

> **Closure** Draw the gift that was originally wished for in workbooks; relax with fleeces.

Dealing with Relationships: Testing & Trusting

12 Who Can I Trust?

 Children  Teenagers

> **Aims** To encourage participants to share their experience about trust and mistrust and to understand the possibility of change.

> **Materials** Large whiteboard, coloured markers, fleeces, mats, large drum(s), personal folders and workbooks, crayons and coloured pens; Worksheets 7 and 8.

Warm Up Invite everyone into the circle and share feedback from previous session. Introduce the theme of trust and how important it is; encourage people to share. Write important words and phrases on the board. Invite the group to choose their favourite warm-up game and two people to lead it.

Activities Group members can colour either Worksheet 7, 'It is Hard to Trust People', or 8, 'Who Can I Trust? (1)', whichever they prefer. Think about the words and phrases on the board:

- ✪ Think about people whom you do not trust and try to remember why.
- ✪ Does this person know you do not trust them?
- ✪ Is it possible to replace them with another person you could trust?
- ✪ Colour or write on one of the worksheets and think how your trust could change.
- ✪ Write something on the worksheet that you would like to tell someone.

> **Sharing** Discuss in the whole group the issues that stop us trusting and mistrusting others.

> **Closure** Draw or write a symbol of trust in workbooks; relax with fleeces.

Dealing with Relationships: Testing & Trusting

13 Being Let Down

 Children  Teenagers

> **Aims** To encourage group members to change from feeling 'let down' to being able to trust.

> **Materials** Large whiteboard, coloured markers, fleeces, mats, large drum(s), personal folders and workbooks, crayons and coloured pens; Worksheet 9.

Warm Up Invite everyone into the circle and share feedback from previous session. Introduce the theme of 'being let down' and how it can affect whether we can trust people or not. Encourage sharing of general examples and write key phrases on the board: for example, forgotten birthdays, changed plans, and so on.

Everyone scatters round the room and jumps as high as possible, then jumps with a partner, and then one person jumps and the other helps them to jump higher.

Activities All of these activities encourage the development of greater trust, although many participants may still be wary:

- ✪ Invite everyone to choose a new partner and take it in turns to lead a run around the room.
- ✪ Stand opposite your partner and hold each other's hands, leaning back to achieve a balance.
- ✪ Slowly move your feet closer towards your partner and then lean back.
- ✪ Finally both pairs of feet touch each other, arms straighten; both partners lean back and achieve perfect balance!
- ✪ Colour and write on Worksheet 9, 'Who Can I Trust? (2)'.

 This exercise needs a lot of trust and capacity to balance. It may need to be done in small stages over more than one session. However, the sense of achievement is palpable once total balance is achieved.

> **Sharing** Encourage group members to think of other potential balancing exercises.

> **Closure** Draw a high tightrope (such as one used in a circus) with a person crossing it; relax with fleeces.

Dealing with Relationships: Testing & Trusting

14 Rock-a-Bye (1)

 Children 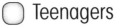 Teenagers

Aims To enable young children to explore 'being dropped', by means of a traditional song.

Materials Large whiteboard, coloured markers, fleeces, mats, large drum(s), personal folders and workbooks, crayons and coloured pens; Story Sheet 2.

Warm Up Invite everyone into the circle and encourage feedback. Introduce the idea of 'being dropped' and give out the words of the song (Story Sheet 2, 'Rock-a-Bye Baby'). Everyone can read or sing them together. Ask for examples of 'being dropped' and write them on the board. Everyone runs around the room; encourage everyone, when the drum beats, to fall to the floor pretending they have been dropped; repeat several times.

Activities These are designed for young children who may relate through the traditional song:

- ✪ Think of all the actions in the song: the rocking of the baby, placing it high up, the cradle rocking, the wind becoming so strong that it breaks the branch, and finally the baby crashing down.
- ✪ Everyone gently picks up the baby and rocks it.
- ✪ Place the baby in a cradle very carefully.
- ✪ Go to the tree and stretch up high, putting the baby in the cradle.
- ✪ Everyone makes wind sounds and sways, more and more strongly.
- ✪ Be the baby crashing down to the floor; repeat with a partner who picks up the baby and then rocks it.

Sharing Talk about how traditional songs and poems can tell us important things about life.

Closure Draw a picture of a safe cradle in workbooks; relax with fleeces.

15 Rock-a-Bye (2)

☑ Children ◯ Teenagers

> **Aims** To assist younger children to understand their own feelings of 'being let down'.

> **Materials** Large whiteboard, coloured markers, fleeces, mats, large drum(s), personal folders and workbooks, crayons and coloured pens; Story Sheet 2.

Warm Up Invite everyone into the circle and share any feedback from previous sessions. Introduce the idea of 'being let down' or 'being dropped'. How does it feel? Write important words on the board. Play touch/no touch games: everyone runs around the room not touching anyone else; repeat, but with everyone lightly touching each other's shoulders as they pass.

Activities Each person needs paper and crayons and a copy of Story Sheet 2, 'Rock-a-Bye Baby'. Invite the group to think about the words of the song. What picture does it suggest?

- ✪ Think about the tree that was used to rock the baby's cradle.
- ✪ Think about what sort of cradle it might have been.
- ✪ Draw a picture of the tree before the branch was broken, while the cradle was still up high.
- ✪ Draw a second tree with the branch broken and the baby and cradle on the ground.
- ✪ Think about a safe place for the baby to be.

> **Sharing** Share the safe place with a partner.

> **Closure** Draw the safe place in workbooks; relax with fleeces.

Dealing with Relationships: Testing & Trusting

16 Living Pictures (1)

◯ Children ☑ Teenagers

Aims To build confidence and communication skills. Activity 15 will be reinforced by Activities 17–21 if participants need to build more confidence.

Materials Large whiteboard, coloured markers, fleeces, mats, large drum(s), personal folders and workbooks, crayons and coloured pens.

Warm Up Invite everyone into the circle and encourage feedback from previous sessions. Introduce the idea of creating a picture with hands, arms and fingers, and suggest some themes (fun, fear, serious, silly, and so on); people can respond with gestures and expressions without leaving their chairs. Allow a release of physical energy through running or jumping.

Activities Start working with the whole group as it allows greater anonymity, then progress to smaller groups, eventually to small groups of three or four.

- Invite people to scatter around the room and stand in their own space, physically apart from everyone else.
- Call out different emotions and ask people to 'freeze' to mime the words: surprise, fear, anger, and so on.
- Develop the words and 'freeze' with a partner: disappointed, proud, disgusted, and so on.
- Create the freeze then, on the drumbeat, change it to the opposite meaning. Make the change slowly, 'melting' from one word to its opposite.
- Jump to come out of the roles and return to oneself.

Sharing Share in the group how it felt to show these feelings and express their opposites. What impact does it have on the body?

Closure Draw an emblem to represent a feeling in workbooks; relax with fleeces.

 ℗ This page may be photocopied for instructional use only. *101 Activities for Social & Emotional Resilience* © Sue Jennings 2013

17 Living Pictures (2)

○ Children   ☑ Teenagers

Aims To develop the physical expression of feelings.

Materials Large whiteboard, coloured markers, fleeces, mats, large drum(s), personal folders and workbooks, crayons and coloured pens; large, strong balloons.

Warm Up Invite everyone into the circle and encourage feedback from previous session. Introduce the idea that not only do we experience feelings in our bodies, we also communicate them to others; blow up two of the balloons and encourage the group to keep them off the ground as long as possible.

Activities Everyone has a balloon and coloured markers:

- ✪ Encourage a breathing exercise as everyone blows up their balloon and knots it.
- ✪ Draw a 'feeling face' on the balloon – write on the board a range of feelings that the group can choose from.
- ✪ Find others who have the same feeling, or the opposite feeling.
- ✪ Create a tableau with others of the feelings that have been drawn on the balloons.
- ✪ Share the tableaux with the whole group.

Sharing In whole group discuss how it felt to express feelings through the body; everyone can safely burst their balloon!

Closure Draw the balloon 'feeling face' in workbooks; relax with fleeces.

18 Insider or Outsider? (1)

☑ Children ◯ Teenagers

Aims To encourage participation with confidence in group activities.

Materials Large whiteboard, coloured markers, fleeces, mats, large drum(s), personal folders and workbooks, crayons and coloured pens; A4 paper for each person, divided up into six circles and numbered 1–6.

Warm Up Invite everyone into the circle and encourage the sharing of feelings from previous sessions; acknowledge that sometimes people feel outside of the group – or the class, or the family. Play a game of chain-tag as a physical warm-up.

Activities Everyone has an A4 sheet of paper with the six circles. Tell the following short tale: 'Lion Cub felt very lonely [circle 1 on the sheets of A4 paper] and all the other young creatures seemed to be happy playing together, laughing and having fun [circle 2]. One day Kite flew over and saw little Lion on his own, and asked him what was the matter. Lion Cub said that he had no playmates and he was lonely [circle 3]. Kite went to see the other small creatures and asked why they did not play with Lion Cub. They said that he was always hiding in the grass and bushes and they never saw him [circle 4]. "Ah," Kite said, "now you know what you could do …"'

- Repeat the story a section at a time (following the numbering above).
- Invite everyone to draw the story of each section in one of their circles.
- Colour each of the pictures, 1–4.
- Think about how the story might end, remembering what Kite has said.
- In circles 5 and 6 create the ending of the story.

Sharing Discuss in the whole group the different endings everyone has drawn for the story.

Closure Draw a frame around your story; relax with fleeces.

19 Insider or Outsider? (2)

○ Children ☑ Teenagers

> **Aims** To encourage participation in group activities.

> **Materials** Large whiteboard, coloured markers, fleeces, mats, large drum(s), personal folders and workbooks, crayons and coloured pens; A4 paper with six circles numbered 1–6.

Warm Up Invite everyone into the group and encourage feedback. Introduce the idea that many stories are about characters who feel on the outside or the inside; share any ideas (from sci-fi stories, and so on) and write them on the board. Warm-up with game of chain-tag.

Activities Everyone has an A4 sheet of paper with the six circles, as well as crayons and coloured pens. Tell the following short story: 'In the great galaxy there is an undiscovered planet whose name will be ... [circle 1], and its inhabitants are known as the ... [circle 2]. The aliens are very strict in their rules and if any young warrior breaks a rule they are rejected from the group [circle 3] and sent to the forest lands, where they have to perform several tasks [circle 4] before being allowed back again ...'

✪ Repeat the story a section at a time (following the numbering above).

✪ Invite everyone to draw each section in one of the circles.

✪ Colour each of the pictures 1–4.

✪ Think about the tasks the alien has to perform and how they will complete them.

✪ In circles 5 and 6 create the ending of the story.

> **Sharing** Discuss in the whole group the different endings for the story.

> **Closure** Draw a frame round your story; relax with fleeces.

Dealing with Relationships: Testing & Trusting

20 Insider or Outsider? (3)

 Children  Teenagers

> **Aims** To progress from storytelling to enactment, for personal insight and understanding.

> **Materials** Large whiteboard, coloured markers, fleeces, mats, large drum(s), personal folders and workbooks, crayons and coloured pens; circle story sheets from previous session.

Warm Up Invite everyone into the circle, and encourage feedback from the picture sessions about 'insider' and 'outsider'; acknowledge everyone's opinions, and any personal statements. Choose a shaking and stretching warm-up.

Activities Everyone looks at their circle story sheet again. People form small groups with whose stories have a similar theme:

- ✪ The groups decide how the stories can be turned into scenes.
- ✪ Explain to the groups the concept of freeze-frames (see Introduction).
- ✪ Illustrate the scenes with four freeze-frames.
- ✪ Show the freeze-frames to the whole group.

> **Sharing** In the small groups, talk about whether the freeze frames could become a drama.

> **Closure** Draw one of the freeze frames in workbooks; relax with fleeces.

Part Three
Building & Maintaining Friendships: Testing the Water

Activities

Worksheets

Story Sheets

Introduction

There are many reasons for children and young people to feel that they do not have friends. They may not have had friends before coming to school, having been an only child, or they may already feel lonely for another reason. They may also have experienced bullying or other unpleasant encounters with their peers. Most children manage to survive the ups and downs of establishing friendships: the experience of making best friends, and having guests for birthday parties, sleepovers, and so on. However, for others it can excruciatingly painful when they are not included in the group, the only one not to be invited home. Maybe they are not in a position to invite others to their home: perhaps it is a foster home that does not allow sleepovers, or there is a relative with mental health issues, or parents who reject contact with outsiders. There are many issues that children and teenagers are unable to change.

The techniques in this section will assist group members to understand the nature of friendship and introduce different ideas for building friendships. Through the use of stories and poems, struggles with friendships and relationships can be seen as issues that affect many of us, rather than just the individual who feels isolated. The structure of this group work enables individuals to slowly acknowledge their needs and to try out friendships within the safety of the group, with leader support. It is an opportunity to practise life and social skills, before testing them in the wider world. It is important at all times to maintain the feeling of safety within the group.

21 Special Friendships

 Children   Teenagers

> **Aims** To encourage insight into friendships and how they can develop.

> **Materials** Large whiteboard, coloured markers, fleeces, mats, large drum(s), personal folders and workbooks, crayons and coloured pens; Worksheets 10 & 11.

Warm Up Invite everyone into the circle and encourage feedback from previous sessions. Open up discussion on the theme of friendship and the difficulties of maintaining friendship. Link to the previous discussion about trust, and write key words for friendship on the board. Make sure the group does an energy-release exercise from the warm-up list in the Introduction.

Activities Continue discussion about friendships and give people a choice of Worksheet 10, 'My Tree of Hearts', or Worksheet 11, 'My Tree of Special People' (girls and younger children usually choose 'My Tree of Hearts').

- Think about friendships of the past and present – what happened to them?
- Colour the worksheet and name special friendships, even if they no longer exist, or friendships that you would like to happen.
- Think hard about why friendships break up and, if there are broken friendships on the sheet, indicate the reason they ended.
- Think hard about anything you may have contributed to the break-up and how it could be put right.
- Think of just one thing that could start or improve a friendship.

> **Sharing** In the whole group, discuss struggles with friendships.

> **Closure** Using workbooks, draw one heart or one circle that could start a new friendship; relax with fleeces.

Building & Maintaining Friendships: Testing the Water

22 A Special Friend (1)

 Children  Teenagers

Aims Supporting group members to identify the reality of friendships.

Materials Large whiteboard, coloured markers, fleeces, mats, large drum(s), personal folders and workbooks, crayons and coloured pens; Story Sheet 3.

Warm Up Invite everyone into the circle and encourage feedback from previous sessions. Suggest that many stories and plays are about friendships and jealousy: people who try to break up friendships. Invite people to contribute ideas from their own viewing or reading, and write ideas on the board. Choose a warm-up that is about holding hands and then breaking away.

Activities Everyone has a copy of Story Sheet 3, a scene from *A Midsummer Night's Dream* in which Helena describes her long friendship with Hermia; explain that it is poetry about friendship, and clarify any words people are unfamiliar with.

- ☺ Read the speech or a section of it.
- ☺ Invite discussion of the different points that Helena makes about friendship.
- ☺ Encourage group members to agree or disagree with Helena's view.
- ☺ Suggest that other words can be added if people choose.
- ☺ Decorate the poem with friendship signs and pictures.

Sharing Discuss the poem with a partner and talk about how Helena must be feeling.

Closure Draw a friendship 'knot' in workbooks; relax with fleeces.

23 A Special Friend (2)

 Children Teenagers

Aims To encourage participants to understand 'what makes a friend'.

Materials Large whiteboard, coloured markers, fleeces, mats, large drum(s), personal folders and workbooks, crayons and coloured pens; Story Sheet 4.

Warm Up Invite group members into the circle and encourage feedback from previous sessions. Continue any discussions about friendships, and special words that make a friendship. Write ideas on the board and invite the group to think about their families as well; do people make friends with members of their families? Explore walking around the room looking open and friendly; then walking around looking closed and distant.

Activities Everyone has a copy of Story Sheet 4, 'The Quarrel'.

- ⊗ Read the poem through twice.
- ⊗ Comment on the rhythm of the poem (you could even follow it with a drumbeat).
- ⊗ Invite comments, which could be about friends, or brothers and sisters.
- ⊗ Suggest that group members create their own poem in the space on Story Sheet 4, as many lines as people wish.
- ⊗ Group members can finish by decorating their poem.

Sharing In pairs, invite people to share their poems and pictures.

Closure Write the name of your poem in your workbook; relax with fleeces.

Building & Maintaining Friendships: Testing the Water

24 Word Game about Friendship (1)

 Children Teenagers

Aims To encourage collaboration in creating new ideas.

Materials Large whiteboard, coloured markers, fleeces, mats, large drum(s), personal folders and workbooks, crayons and coloured pens.

Warm Up Invite everyone into the circle and encourage feedback from previous sessions. Suggest everyone plays word games and calls out words connected with friendship, which are then written on the board. Repeat the physical warm-up from Activity 23.

Activities Introduce the idea that group members will work together to create a poem or some sayings about friendship.

- ✪ Write the word 'friendship' vertically on the board (or just 'friend' for younger group members).
- ✪ Work in pairs with workbooks and write a phrase beside each letter of the word 'friendship'.
- ✪ Think about whether the words are turning into a poem with a rhythm.
- ✪ Make sure the pairs give each other enough time to come up with ideas.

Sharing Encourage the pairs to read out their 'poem' to the whole group.

Closure Write the first line of your poem in your workbook; relax with fleeces.

  P This page may be photocopied for instructional use only. *101 Activities for Social & Emotional Resilience* © Sue Jennings 2013

25 Word Game about Friendship (2)

☑ Children   ☑ Teenagers

Aims To stimulate group collaboration in creating new ideas.

Materials Large whiteboard, coloured markers, fleeces, mats, large drum(s), personal folders and workbooks, crayons and coloured pens.

Warm Up The same warm-up as Activity 24, as this is a variation of the same exercise.

Activities Write the word 'friendship' vertically on the whiteboard (or 'friend' for younger groups); use a variety of coloured pens.

- ✪ People call out possible phrases that start with each letter.
- ✪ Include alternatives that come from a variety of participants.
- ✪ Try very short lines of one or two words.
- ✪ Encourage rhythm.
- ✪ Write out the poem(s) and copy them for everyone.

Sharing Discuss the variation in the different suggestions.

Closure Write the word 'friend' in workbooks and colour it; relax with fleeces.

Building & Maintaining Friendships: Testing the Water

26 # Special Words for Special People

☑ Children ☑ Teenagers

Aims To identify qualities that might be valued in a friendship.

Materials Large whiteboard, coloured markers, fleeces, mats, large drum(s), personal folders and workbooks, crayons and coloured pens; Worksheet 12.

Warm Up Invite group members into the circle and encourage feedback from previous sessions. Suggest a discussion about the qualities that individual group members possess that are admired by others, and whether these qualities would contribute to a friendship. Spend some time walking briskly around the room, and then calling out names; first the individual calls out their own name, then the whole group echoes the name.

Activities Everyone has a copy of Worksheet 12, 'Special Words for a Special Friend', and can use the ideas generated in the warm-up to fill in the spaces.

✪ Colour in the circles that you feel contain important qualities for friends.

✪ Think of other qualities that are important and write these in the blank circles.

✪ Write on the chart positive qualities group members feel they have.

✪ Write down any qualities that you need to be careful about, because they could affect a friendship.

✪ Decorate the whole sheet.

Sharing Share and compare worksheets with a partner, and discuss similarities and differences.

Closure Write the most important quality in workbooks; relax with fleeces.

27 Friendship Badges

 Children  Teenagers

Aims	To encourage participants to create symbols of friendship.

Materials	Large whiteboard, coloured markers, fleeces, mats, large drum(s), personal folders and workbooks, crayons and coloured, fine-point felt-tip pens; large white cardboard badges with safety pins attached at the back.

Warm Up   Invite everyone into the circle and encourage feedback from previous sessions. Continue discussions about the nature of friendship, and consider whether people are more aware of the meaning of friendship as a result of the previous sessions. Choose a physical warm-up to generate energy.

Activities   Before distributing the badges, discuss ideas about friendship and how these could be portrayed in a picture. Invite everyone to create a 'badge of friendship', using coloured felt-tip pens with fine points.

- ✪ Choose colours to create the badge.
- ✪ Decide on a symbol or sign that shows friendship.
- ✪ Allow for rushed and messy pictures, and second goes.
- ✪ Suggest that this could be the badge of a friendship club.
- ✪ Allow everyone to wear their badges.

Sharing	Show and share badges in the whole group.

Closure	Draw your friendship symbol in your workbook; relax with fleeces.

28 Knot of Friendship

☑ Children ☑ Teenagers

Aims To affirm potential for making and keeping friends.

Materials Large whiteboard, coloured markers, fleeces, mats, large drum(s), personal folders and workbooks, crayons and coloured pens; Worksheet 13.

Warm Up Invite everyone into the circle and encourage feedback from previous sessions. Suggest that people have experienced many dimensions of friendship, and invite individuals to share what they have learnt about it. Ask everyone to form two groups; each group pretends to hold onto one end of an imaginary rope that runs between the groups. Find a way for the two groups to balance themselves at each end of the imaginary rope.

Activities Discuss some images of ropes and knots, such as 'tying the knot' or friendship knots and bracelets. Everyone has Worksheet 13, 'My Special Friend (1)', and coloured pens.

- ✪ Each person thinks of a friend with whom they have a strong friendship, or someone they would like to have as a friend.
- ✪ Colour the knotted rope in an individual way to describe the friendship.
- ✪ Make sure the knot itself is emphasised.
- ✪ Write or draw the special qualities of your friend underneath the knot.
- ✪ Write or draw the special qualities you can offer to your friend.

Sharing Show the whole group the knots and share the qualities.

Closure Draw a knotted circle in workbooks; relax with fleeces.

---

29 Picture of a Friend

 Children Teenagers

Aims To allow participants to create the reality or fantasy of a special friend.

Materials Large whiteboard, coloured markers, fleeces, mats, large drum(s), personal folders and workbooks, crayons and coloured pens; Worksheet 14.

Warm Up Invite everyone into the group and encourage feedback from previous sessions. Continue the discussion about the qualities of friends. What don't we like in our friends? Suggest that group members, in pairs, start to choose the physical warm-ups themselves (see Introduction).

Activities Everyone has a copy of Worksheet 14, 'My Special Friend' (2), and crayons and pens.

- ❂ Invite group members to close their eyes and think about a friend they really have – or one they would like to have.
- ❂ What does their face look like?
- ❂ Are there special features that friends have?
- ❂ Draw the friend's portrait in the frame on the worksheet.
- ❂ Colour and decorate the picture.

Sharing Stick all the pictures on the whiteboard so that everyone may see the 'portrait gallery'.

Closure Write or draw one feature that is important in a friend in workbooks; relax with fleeces.

30 A Friendship Club

 Children  Teenagers

Aims To encourage group members to get together and share things in common.

Materials Large whiteboard, coloured markers, fleeces, mats, large drum(s), personal folders and workbooks, crayons and coloured pens; large white badges with safety pins at the back.

Warm Up Invite everyone into the group and encourage feedback from previous sessions. Introduce the idea of groups of friends and how they can share things in common. Group members are invited to choose a physical warm-up.

Activities Continue the idea of people sharing things in common, including hobbies, sports and special foods.

- ✪ Invite suggestions for special interests and write them on the board.
- ✪ Group the ideas into activities such sports, dance, outdoors.
- ✪ Create sub-groups around things that people might collect.
- ✪ Everyone creates a badge for a club they would like to join.
- ✪ Encourage the group to be one large friendship club, which also contains smaller groups with special interests.

 Some children and teenagers may not have existing interests, and may discover a new hobby while in the group. This session needs to be flexible in order to accommodate the variation in people's experience. Maybe a new initiative can develop out of this session, leading to the creation of special interest groups? This will also reinforce friendships.

Sharing Encourage partners to share things in common.

Closure Draw a special interest in workbooks; relax with fleeces.

Part Four
Self-Control & Self-Respect: Rhythms for Change

Activities

Introduction

When parents or teachers shout at a teenager or child, 'Control yourself!', they are usually asking the impossible. The out-of-control child is usually in a very scary place, and there is nothing they would like more than to be able to control themselves. Whether in its mildest form (always interrupting, being unable to wait one's turn), or in its most extreme form (a full-scale tantrum), lack of self-control is often linked to fear, frustration or chaotic lifestyle. When a young person is out of control, the chemical balance of their brain is upset, and they will not be able to reassert control until this imbalance has corrected itself. Parents can shorten these episodes by tight holding and containing (more difficult if the teenager is larger than you are!). In the group there can be skilled use of the fleece as a way of wrapping up and feeling boundaries.

The following techniques mainly focus on the use of rhythm: the out-of-control individual has usually lost their personal 'rhythm of life', and by the use of drumming and rhythm work it is possible to regain self-control. Gradually, repetitive rhythms with drums and voice are internalised, and make a direct impact on the nervous system. These activities could be compared to the early rhythmic experience of small babies, who are rocked and cradled while listening to nursery rhymes such as 'Pat-a-cake'. Chants in fairy stories have regular, repetitive rhythms: 'I'll huff, and I'll puff, and I'll blow your house down!' Many out-of-control children and teenagers have not had these important early experiences. The following techniques help to redress the balance.

31 Drumming for Living (1)

 Children Teenagers

Aims To build up self-confidence through drumming in synchronicity.

Materials Large whiteboard, coloured markers, fleeces, mats, large drum(s), personal folders and workbooks, crayons and coloured pens.

Warm Up Invite everyone into the circle and encourage feedback from previous sessions. Introduce the word 'control', and ask the group to suggest what it means. Write the suggestions on the board. Invite everyone to find things in the room to use to make rhythms: the floor, walls, doors, their hands, and so on. Let the sounds they make become very loud … and then, slowly, quieter and quieter.

Activities Using the drum to lead the rhythm, encourage group members to engage with rhythms in the room (perhaps suggesting that during a later session they might use drums and other percussion instruments).

⊗ Beat a slow rhythm on the drum and invite group members to follow you.

⊗ Increase the complexity by making a strong beat followed by a light beat.

⊗ Gradually increase the pace, making sure everyone can keep up.

⊗ Slow the pace again, and keep a group rhythm.

⊗ Slow to a very quiet and gentle rhythm.

Sharing Sit with a partner and create a rhythm together.

Closure Sit back to back with a partner and be aware of heartbeats; relax with fleeces.

Self-Control & Self-Respect: Rhythms for Change

32 Drumming for Living (2)

 Children  Teenagers

Aims To encourage self-control through understanding body rhythms.

Materials Large whiteboard, coloured markers, fleeces, mats, large drum(s), personal folders and workbooks, crayons and coloured pens.

Warm Up Invite everyone into the circle and encourage feedback from previous sessions. Continue to discuss control and how self-control might bring greater freedom. Invite everyone to feel their pulse and comment on their personal rhythms.

Activities Invite group members to find a space in the room; use the drum to establish start and finish.

- Beat out rhythms on the chest (body percussion).
- Repeat and add vocal sound ('Tarzan' calls).
- Discover other rhythms, using hands, stomachs, thighs, and so on.
- Put a rhythm programme together, structured by the drum.
- Create a 'body' orchestra and explore different sounds, finishing each sound with a slow and quiet rhythm.

Sharing Give feedback in the group by using rhythms and sounds, not words.

Closure Sit back to back with partner and be aware of both heartbeats; relax with fleeces.

33 Clapping & Confidence

☑ Children ☑ Teenagers

Aims To build self-confidence through successful rhythmic participation.

Materials Large whiteboard, coloured markers, fleeces, mats, personal folders and workbooks, crayons and coloured pens.

Warm Up Invite everyone into the circle, and acknowledge that any feedback will be welcome later. Standing in the circle, ask the whole group to clap at the same time, starting slowly, getting faster, and then more slowly again.

Activities Invite the group to sit or stand in the circle:

- ✪ Continuing the warm-up, everyone claps together.
- ✪ Introduce a new rhythm (ta, ta, ta-ta-ta, for example) while the steady clapping continues.
- ✪ Encourage volunteers to introduce a rhythm during the clapping.
- ✪ Continue with the steady clapping while individuals try out their own rhythms.
- ✪ If the group is confident, encourage the whole group to follow someone's individual rhythm.

Sharing In the whole group encourage feedback about any of the rhythmic work.

Closure Draw around hands in workbooks and colour; relax with fleeces.

Self-Control & Self-Respect: Rhythms for Change

34 Massage & Back Drumming

 Children Teenagers

Aims To develop confidence and trust through body touch.

Materials Large whiteboard, coloured markers, fleeces, mats, large drum(s), personal folders and workbooks, crayons and coloured pens.

Warm Up Invite everyone into the circle, and acknowledge that some people find touch difficult. Explain that the only 'safe-touch' areas are the back – shoulders to waist – and the hands. Everyone stands in a line, one behind the other, and uses the flat of one hand to make a big circle on the back of the person in front.

Activities Invite the group to stand in a line and explore the following touch exercises:

- Put hands on the shoulders of the person in front, and massage the shoulders with thumbs.
- Repeat big circles on people's backs.
- Use very light karate chops across the shoulder and down the back to the waist.
- Use the flat of the hands to lightly beat across the back.
- Turn around and repeat the four exercises on the back of the person on the other side.

Sharing Discuss in the whole group any feelings of discomfort and how to overcome them.

Closure Sit back to back with a partner and deep breathe; close eyes and relax with fleeces.

35 High Five!

✓ Children ✓ Teenagers

Aims To build up focus and rhythms in the group.

Materials Large whiteboard, coloured markers, fleeces, mats, large drum(s), personal folders and workbooks, crayons and coloured pens.

Warm Up Invite everyone into a standing circle and explain that feedback will be shared later in the group. Pass a 'high five' around the group, starting slowly and increasing pace; then pass it in the opposite direction.

Activities Continue in the standing circle, and build on the skills of the warm-up:

- ✪ Pass a clap round the group, and let the speed build up; send it in opposite direction.
- ✪ Pass a double-clap round the group, increasing the speed; send it in the opposite direction.
- ✪ Throw an imaginary ball round the group, saying 'to you' as it is thrown.
- ✪ Repeat, but this time anyone can call out 'to me'. The ball is thrown to that person, still saying 'to you'.
- ✪ Repeat, but if 'back again' is called out, the ball has to be thrown in the opposite direction.

It is very important that this type of game is not set up for people to fail. Many participants may be uncoordinated, have slow reactions and some may even panic. The exercise needs to be done gradually, with repetitions, until the whole group can move to the more complex stage.

Sharing In the whole group, invite feedback from this and previous sessions.

Closure Sit back to back with a partner and deep breathe; close eyes and relax with fleeces.

36 Waves of the Sea

☑ Children   ◯ Teenagers

Aims To develop concentration and group cooperation.

Materials Large whiteboard, coloured markers, fleeces, mats, large drum(s), personal folders and workbooks, crayons and coloured pens.

Warm Up Invite everyone into the standing circle, and explain that discussion will take place later. Pass a 'high five' around the group, slowly at first and then speed it up; send it in the opposite direction.

Activities Continue in the circle and build on the skills of the warm-up:

- ✪ Call out 'waves', and everyone makes sea-wave movements with their arms.
- ✪ Call out 'storm', and everyone has to stamp their feet.
- ✪ Call out 'shipwreck', and everyone lies flat on the floor.
- ✪ Repeat with variations until the group is working together.
- ✪ Pass the wave movement around the group until someone calls 'storm' or 'shipwreck'; then start the wave movement in the opposite direction.

Sharing Discuss in the group other possible variations, and try them out if there is time.

Closure Sit back to back with a partner and deep breathe; close eyes and relax with fleeces.

37 Percussion Ritual (1)

☑ Children ☑ Teenagers

> **Aims**   To develop the rhythms of the group in a collaborative way.

> **Materials**   Drum or tambour for each group member.

Warm Up   Invite everyone into a sitting circle and encourage feedback from previous sessions. Explain that the session will focus on drumming and rhythms. Drumming the hands on the floor or the thighs, pass a simple rhythm round the circle, then repeat it all together three times; repeat with another rhythm passed in the opposite direction.

Activities   Everyone sits in a circle with their own drum or tambour. Explain that the instruments are only to be used for drumming, and no excessive force is required.

- ✪ Echo rhythm: play a simple rhythm that the group repeats.
- ✪ Pass a simple rhythm around the circle, and slowly speed it up.
- ✪ Invite individuals to start a rhythm that is repeated by the whole group together and then passed around the circle.
- ✪ Create a sequence that involves everyone's rhythms.
- ✪ Repeat the sequence, including both group rhythms performed together, as well as rhythms passed round the circle.

> **Sharing**   With a partner, have a conversation using the drum or tambour instead of words.

> **Closure**   Very lightly, use fingertips to create a soothing sound on the drum; relax with fleeces.

Self-Control & Self-Respect: Rhythms for Change

38 Percussion Ritual (2)

 Children  Teenagers

Aims To build up coordination through rhythm and movement.

Materials Large whiteboard, coloured markers, fleeces, mats, large drum(s), personal folders and workbooks, crayons and coloured pens; enough drums for half the group members.

Warm Up Invite everyone into the standing circle, and explain they are building on their drumming skills and rhythms. Start a stamping rhythm all together (like marching on the spot); vary the rhythm with light and strong beats.

Activities The group stays in the standing circle and builds on the warm-up:

- Everyone stamps four times, and then shouts 'ha!'
- Practise the chant 'ha, ah, ah, ah!' (starting on one note, then down a note, then up a note, then back to the first note).
- Slow stamps while chanting together.
- Half the group make the rhythm on the drum, the other half sway and chant.
- Change over so everyone has a chance to drum.

Sharing Discuss with a partner your preference between chanting and drumming.

Closure Draw a drum in workbooks; relax with fleeces.

39 Follow the Rhythm (1)

☑ Children ☑ Teenagers

Aims To increase focus and awareness of group dynamics.

Materials Large whiteboard, coloured markers, fleeces, mats, large drum(s), personal folders and workbooks, crayons and coloured pens.

Warm Up Invite everyone into the standing circle and ask for a volunteer to be 'leader'; they perform an action and everyone else follows, copying the actions; change leaders several times.

Activities Everyone returns to the standing circle, leaving plenty of space between themselves and others. Explain that this game is about being alert to other people's movements:

- ✪ One person at a time takes a step into the circle.
- ✪ If more than one person steps in at the same time, then the game starts again.
- ✪ The games finishes when each person has stepped once into the circle.
- ✪ There will be frustration and sighs, and stop–starts!
- ✪ There will be a great sense of satisfaction when the whole group manages to step in sequence.

Sharing In the group share frustrations and pleasure at the exercise, and any previous exercises.

Closure Sit back to back with a partner, practise deep breathing, and relax on fleeces.

---

40 Follow the Rhythm (2)

 Children  Teenagers

Aims To further increase focus and collaboration within the group.

Materials Large whiteboard, coloured markers, fleeces, mats, large drum(s), personal folders and workbooks, crayons and coloured pens.

Warm Up Invite everyone into a standing circle, and ask group members to choose and lead rhythmic warm-ups.

Activities Everyone continues in the standing circle:

- ⊗ One person at a time sits down.
- ⊗ If more than one person sits down at the same time, the game starts again.
- ⊗ The games finishes when everyone has sat down in sequence.
- ⊗ The game is really completed when everyone is also able to stand up in sequence.
- ⊗ This game can be repeated, because once success is achieved, the participants experience a real sense of well-being.

Sharing In the group, share feelings of 'well-being' from different exercises.

Closure Sit back to back, breathe deeply and relax on fleeces.

Part Five
Building Confidence: Creating the Safety Net

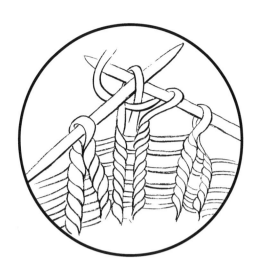

Activities

Worksheets

41 Feeling Good about Myself (1)

☑ Children   ☑ Teenagers

Aims To build personal skills that develop confidence.

Materials Large whiteboard, coloured markers, fleeces, mats, large drum(s), personal folders and workbooks, crayons and coloured pens.

Warm Up Invite everyone into the circle and encourage participants to share how they would like to feel more confident. Write key words on the board. Encourage group members to suggest and lead a physical exercise to warm up the group.

Activities Bring everyone into a standing circle:

⊗ Hold hands and encourage the group to pull and push without breaking the circle.

⊗ Still holding hands, lift the arms; everyone threads through the group to begin to form a human knot.

⊗ Lower the arms and everyone climbs over each other's arms to make the knot tighter.

⊗ Focus on tightening the knot with hands still held firmly.

⊗ Take time to undo the knot without breaking the circle! This becomes a mathematical problem, especially when the group ends up facing outwards instead of inwards!

Sharing Invite members to suggest more physical exercises.

Closure Draw a positive symbol in workbooks that gives confidence; relax with fleeces.

42 Feeling Good about Myself (2)

☑ Children ☑ Teenagers

> **Aims** To continue to build personal skills.

> **Materials** Large whiteboard, coloured markers, fleeces, mats, personal folders and workbooks, crayons and coloured pens.

Warm Up Invite everyone into a standing circle, hold hands firmly and test if the circle holds. Quickly continue feedback around issues regarding personal confidence, and write key words on the board.

Activities If the group needs a more physical warm-up, suggest they scatter and run around the room:

- Choose a partner who is more or less the same height.
- The partners put their hands on each other's shoulders and try to push each other across the room.
- Show that by increasing the downward force of the legs, it is less easy to be pushed.
- Create a mock struggle by alternating the pushes between partners.
- Find perfect balance so that no one can push their partner backwards, perhaps by leaning into each other.

> **Sharing** Discuss with a partner any changes in self-confidence.

> **Closure** Partners share the symbols that give them confidence; relax with fleeces.

Building Confidence: Creating the Safety Net

43 Feeling Good about Myself (3)

☑ Children ☑ Teenagers

> **Aims** To develop more personal skills and confidence.

> **Materials** Large whiteboard, coloured markers, fleeces, mats, large drum(s), personal folders and workbooks, crayons and coloured pens.

Warm Up Invite everyone into a sitting circle, and encourage feedback about any changes in personal confidence. Write key words on the board. Suggest group members choose a physical warm-up.

Activities Use a scattering and running around the room exercise to encourage physical energy and focus:

- ✪ Choose a partner who is more or less the same height.
- ✪ Hold hands with the partner, and try grip the floor with the feet.
- ✪ Without jerking movements, try to pull the partner across the room.
- ✪ Create a mock struggle by alternating the pulling between partners.
- ✪ Find a perfect balance in pairs so no one is able to pull their partner.

> **Sharing** Everyone tries their strength by arm-wrestling their partner.

> **Closure** Write one positive word for confidence in workbooks; relax with fleeces.

44 Shield of Protection (1)

☑ Children ☑ Teenagers

> **Aims** To build up strengths to improve confidence.

> **Materials** Large whiteboard, coloured markers, fleeces, mats, large drum(s), personal folders and workbooks, crayons and coloured pens; Worksheet 15.

Warm Up Invite everyone into the circle and encourage feedback from previous sessions. Introduce the idea of self-protection, and the qualities that are needed. Write ideas on the board. Suggest group members choose and lead a physical warm-up.

Activities Each person has Worksheet 15, 'My Shield of Protection (that others can see)', crayons and coloured pens:

- ✪ Explain that the outside of the shield protects the person behind it.
- ✪ Divide the shield horizontally into two parts, and draw a personal emblem in the top half.
- ✪ Write a personal motto in the bottom half, using old-fashioned lettering.
- ✪ Decorate the motto and the emblem, choosing matching colours.
- ✪ Decorate the whole shield with strong colours and patterns.

> **Sharing** Put all the shields up on the board and allow time for sharing their similarities and differences.

> **Closure** Write personal mottos in workbooks; relax with fleeces.

Building Confidence: Creating the Safety Net

45 Shield of Protection (2)

 Children Teenagers

Aims To develop more complex self-protective strengths.

Materials Large whiteboard, coloured markers, fleeces, mats, large drum(s), personal folders and workbooks, crayons and coloured pens; Worksheet 15.

Warm Up Invite everyone into the circle and encourage feedback from previous sessions. Continue the discussion of self-protection, and invite more ideas for symbols and mottos.

Activities Everyone has Worksheet 15, 'My Shield of Protection (that others can see)', as well as crayons and coloured pens:

- ✪ Divide the shield into four parts and write your personal motto across the top.
- ✪ Choose four symbols to represent protection and personal strength. The symbols can include: animals, plants, trees, people, eyes, hearts, hands, and so on.
- ✪ Draw a symbol in each of the four sections.
- ✪ Colour the whole shield and the symbols.

Sharing Put all the shields up on the board, and discuss their similarities and differences.

Closure Draw and colour a favourite symbol in workbooks; relax with fleeces.

46 Personal Strengths (1)

✓ Children   ✓ Teenagers

> **Aims** To support individuals to acknowledge their personal qualities.

> **Materials** Large whiteboard, coloured markers, fleeces, mats, large drum(s), personal folders and workbooks, crayons and coloured pens; Worksheet 16.

Warm Up Invite everyone into a circle and encourage feedback from previous sessions. Introduce the theme of personal and coping strengths, and write any key words on the board. Group members choose a physical warm-up.

Activities Allow some time for reflection to encourage people to think about personal qualities that help them feel more confident. Everyone has Worksheet 16, 'My Shield of Protection (that only I can see)', and crayons and pens:

- ✪ The worksheet is the inside of the shield.
- ✪ Think about what could be written and drawn on the inside to encourage confidence.
- ✪ Write one saying that would be helpful.
- ✪ Draw one symbol that would give strength.
- ✪ Colour the pictures; connect the pictures and writing.

> **Sharing** Share with a partner, and remember this may be confidential, personal information.

> **Closure** Everyone writes their most important quality in their workbook; relax with fleeces.

Building Confidence: Creating the Safety Net

47 Personal Strengths (2)

 Children Teenagers

Aims To encourage naming and recognising personal strengths.

Materials Old newspapers, magazines, glue, scissors, Worksheet 16.

Warm Up Invite everyone into the circle and encourage feedback from previous sessions. Continue acknowledging personal qualities and write ideas on the board. Encourage group members to choose a physical warm-up.

Activities Everyone has a copy of Worksheet 16, 'My Shield of Protection (that only I can see)', as well as newspapers, magazines, scissors, glue:

- ❂ Cut out pictures of people who have positive qualities.
- ❂ Cut out pictures of people who have achieved something inspiring.
- ❂ Cut out words that make statements of hope.
- ❂ Stick them on the reverse of the shield as a collage of inspiration.
- ❂ Colour any gaps and create a frame for the collage.

Sharing Put all the pictures up on the board and look at their similarities and differences.

Closure Write the most important name or word in workbooks; relax with fleeces.

48 Personal Strengths (3)

☑ Children ☑ Teenagers

Aims To identify personal strengths for dealing with difficulties or a crisis.

Materials Large whiteboard, coloured markers, fleeces, mats, large drum(s), personal folders and workbooks, crayons and coloured pens, A4 paper.

Warm Up Invite everyone into the circle and encourage feedback from previous sessions. Discuss different qualities that people have identified in pictures, and write these on the board. Group members choose a physical warm-up.

Activities Everyone needs A4 paper, crayons and coloured pens. Continue the discussion of personal qualities for dealing with difficulties or a crisis:

⊗ Invite everyone to draw six circles on their paper.

⊗ Write the following words on the board: feelings, thoughts, beliefs, friends, imagination and physical activity.

⊗ Give examples of coping in a crisis: some people become very logical, others show their feelings, others need their friends ... and so on.

⊗ Suggest that everyone writes one of the words in each circle, and then colours in the one that is most important to them.

⊗ Consider the other words and whether they are important for coping.

Sharing With the whole group, identify which qualities have been preferred by the majority of people.

Closure Write your own most important strength in your workbook; relax with fleeces.

Building Confidence: Creating the Safety Net

49 Personal Strengths (4a)

☑ Children ☑ Teenagers

> **Aims** To support individuals in their choice of strong role models to copy.

> **Materials** Large whiteboard, coloured markers, fleeces, mats, large drum(s), personal folders and workbooks, crayons and coloured pens, A4 paper.

Warm Up Invite everyone into the circle and encourage feedback from previous sessions. Discuss whether qualities can be learned through practice. Write suggestions on the board. The group chooses a physical warm-up.

Activities Everyone needs A4 paper, crayons and coloured pens. Invite each person to divide their piece of paper into six sections of equal size. Number them in sequence, 1–6. Read through all the instructions before the group starts:

- ✪ Think of a character or person who is central to a story, either imaginary or someone who actually exists. Where do they live? (1)
- ✪ Think of a task or mission the character has to fulfil. (2)
- ✪ Think of something that is stopping them achieving their goal. (3)
- ✪ Does the character have any helpers? (4)
- ✪ What happens next? (5)
- ✪ What is the most important coping strength that the character can use to complete their task? How does the whole story end? (6)
- ✪ Repeat the instructions, one stage at a time, and everyone fills in the boxes. The boxes can be written or drawn in – or both.
- ✪ Write your story down in workbooks without using the pictures as a prompt.

> **Sharing** Read out the story to a partner, and compare ideas.

> **Closure** Draw and colour characters in workbooks; relax with fleeces.

50 Personal Strengths (4b)

✓ Children   ✓ Teenagers

Aims To look in depth at people's coping strengths.

Materials Large whiteboard, coloured markers, fleeces, mats, large drum(s), personal folders and workbooks, crayons and coloured pens; stories from the previous session.

Warm Up Invite everyone into the circle and share any thoughts after the stories thought of during the previous session. Group members can choose a physical warm-up.

Activities Everyone has their A4 story sheet with the six boxes from the previous session.

- ✪ Look through the story boxes and then rewrite your story from memory in workbooks.
- ✪ Read through the story in the workbook and compare it with the story boxes from the last session.
- ✪ Did the story agree with the picture boxes for the character's main coping strength?
- ✪ Work with a partner and compare stories and picture boxes.
- ✪ With partners give feedback to each other about coping.
- ✪ With partners share coping skills they would like to develop.

Sharing Discuss in the whole group ideas for developing coping strengths.

Closure Write or draw the most important coping strength in workbooks; relax with fleeces.

Part Six
Families:
All Sorts & Sizes

Activities

Worksheets

Story Sheets

Introduction

There are many ways of addressing family issues in a group without any focus on the actual families of the participants. Some children or teenagers may wish to share personal information, and decisions need to be made regarding whether this is appropriate. Disclosures need to be acknowledged (without being explored) and group members should be aware of confidentiality. It may be that a referral needs to be made to the school counsellor. Most of the work in this section is done through stories, texts and worksheets about a fictional family. Participants are encouraged to have a dream family, which can be a source of support when the world looks bleak.

The techniques dealing with relationships and friendships are also useful in relation to the family focus, and many children and teenagers feel supported by discovering they can make new friends. Individuals may also experience some hope when they realise that other people have similar families to their own.

Participants will come from a variety of family situations: single parent, step-families, care homes, foster and adoptive families, or may live with grandparents or older siblings. In building up resilience, it important to encourage the development of coping skills that deal with 'difference'.

51 My Family

☑ Children ☑ Teenagers

Aims To encourage participants to see themselves in context of the extended family.

Materials Large whiteboard, coloured markers, fleeces, mats, large drum(s), personal folders and workbooks, crayons and coloured pens; Worksheets 17 & 18.

Warm Up Invite everyone into the circle and welcome feedback. Introduce the theme of families, and the fact that there are many different types of family (see Part Six introductory notes). Mention that we all use different names for family members, and invite the group to give (for example) the name everyone uses for their grandmother; write all the variations on the board.

Activities It is important to normalise this exercise by talking about the way in which some people have 'old' families and some have 'new' families; allow group members to choose between Worksheet 17, 'My Family Tree' and 18, 'My New Family Tree'.

- ✪ Colour in the leaf person that is you.
- ✪ Colour in mums and dads; alternatively, colour in a mum *or* a dad.
- ✪ Think about grannies and grandads; what colours do they wear?
- ✪ Who else is on your tree? Maybe cousins? Aunties? Colour in the people you can remember.
- ✪ Colour the tree itself – this is your Family Tree.

Obviously any work on the theme of families should be undertaken with care. However, acknowledging all of the variation in families is helpful for children and teenagers who feel they are different. Carefully note any disclosures or causes for concern.

Sharing Encourage group members to share their family tree with a friend or discuss their trees in the whole group.

Closure Draw a tree of your own, with blossoms and leaves, in workbooks; relax with fleeces.

Families: All Sorts & Sizes

52 My Dream Family

 Children  Teenagers

Aims To encourage group members to think about the families they could have if they had a choice.

Materials Large whiteboard, coloured markers, fleeces, mats, large drum(s), personal folders and workbooks, crayons and coloured pens; Worksheet 19.

Warm Up Invite everyone into the circle and encourage feedback about previous sessions. Introduce the idea that some people may not live with their families, not through their own fault, and that it is fine to have dream families. Encourage discussion of what a dream family might be like.

Activities Everyone has Worksheet 19, 'My Dream Family', and crayons and coloured pens.

- ✪ Think about dream people.
- ✪ Who would be good to have in your family?
- ✪ Colour the leaves as dream people.
- ✪ Colour the tree so it is individual to you.
- ✪ Put yourself in your dream family.

Sharing Talk in the whole group about dreams and families.

Closure Using workbooks, draw or write something important that you can give to a family; relax with fleeces.

53 My Family of Hearts

 Children  Teenagers

> **Aims** To encourage people to express their feelings about families in a safe environment.

> **Materials** Large whiteboard, coloured markers, fleeces, mats, large drum(s), personal folders and workbooks, crayons and coloured pens; Worksheet 10.

Warm Up Invite everyone into the group and encourage feedback. Continue the theme of families that one hopes for, and whether people can also change if they find themselves in their 'hoped-for' family. The group chooses a warm-up.

Activities Each person has Worksheet 10, 'My Tree of Hearts', crayons and coloured pens.

- ✪ Introduce the idea that the phrase 'if only' is not helpful, giving examples: 'If only my family would change, then I would be happier'; or, 'If only I looked cool, then I would have lots of friends.'

- ✪ Everyone thinks about the times when they might use or have used the phrase 'if only'.

- ✪ Using Worksheet 10, each person writes and colours on several hearts to show the qualities they have to give a family.

- ✪ Write and colour several hearts to show the qualities that other people might need in order to be positive members of the Heart Family.

- ✪ Make sure that one heart is coloured in for 'Trust'!

> **Sharing** Talk with a partner about the hearts and share your pictures.

> **Closure** Draw one heart in workbooks and write something positive inside; relax with fleeces.

Families: All Sorts & Sizes

54 **Dancing Grandmas**

 Children  Teenagers

> **Aims** To assist children and teenagers to be aware of older people and the fact that they can be a source of support.

> **Materials** Large whiteboard, coloured markers, fleeces, mats, large drum(s), personal folders and workbooks, crayons and coloured pens; CD of rhythmic music, CD player.

Warm Up Invite everyone into the circle and encourage feedback, both about previous sessions and also about how people are feeling right now. Introduce the theme of grandmas and invite any comments about them. Suggest everyone walks around the room as a grandma or grandpa: they can really exaggerate this, walking slowly or with a stoop and greeting each other in old voices. Then everyone thinks of an old person who is active and moves as they move.

Activities This exercise needs plenty of space for everyone to move around. Invite everyone to lie flat on their fleece and close their eyes. Ask the group to:

- ✪ 'Imagine you are growing older, and your movement is getting slower.'
- ✪ 'Slowly sit up, and then stand and fold up your fleece.'
- ✪ 'Walk around the room as if you are an old person, perhaps with a stick.'
- ✪ 'When the music starts, suddenly those limbs can move, and you can dance!' [Suggested music: Abba's 'Dancing Queen', or another favourite rhythmic pop tune.]
- ✪ 'Keep dancing and find a partner to dance with, until the music stops.'

> **Sharing** Talk in the whole group about how it felt to really dance!

> **Closure** Draw and colour a dancing grandma or grandpa in workbooks; relax with fleeces.

Families: All Sorts & Sizes

55 The Hunchback in the Park

☑ Children ☑ Teenagers

> **Aims** To encourage awareness of older people and their dreams.

> **Materials** Large whiteboard, coloured markers, fleeces, mats, large drum(s), personal folders and workbooks, crayons and coloured pens; Story Sheet 5.

Warm Up Invite everyone into the circle and share feedback from previous session. Discuss any thoughts about grandparents and older people. What do old people think about when they are on their own? Repeat warm-up from Activity 54, developing the idea of older people and how they move. Then everyone holds hands in a circle and gallops to the right, and then to the left, without letting go. Slowly everyone adjusts to the same pace.

Activities Everyone has a copy of Story Sheet 5, 'The Hunchback in the Park', a poem by Dylan Thomas.

- ✪ Read the poem slowly to the group, and explain any unfamiliar words.
- ✪ Invite comments about the poem.
- ✪ Read the poem again with different individuals reading a line each.
- ✪ Discuss how realistic the poem is; would this situation happen?
- ✪ Everyone illustrates their sheet with ideas from the poem such as trees, children, an old man, flowers, park gates, and so on.

> **Sharing** Share thoughts and pictures in the whole group.

> **Closure** Draw flowing water in workbooks; relax with fleeces.

56 **What do Grandmas Do?**

☑ Children   ☑ Teenagers

Aims To encourage reflection about older people and to consider relationships with them.

Materials Large whiteboard, coloured markers, fleeces, mats, large drum(s), personal folders and workbooks, crayons and coloured pens; Story Sheet 6.

Warm Up Invite everyone into the circle and encourage feedback from previous sessions. Introduce the theme of relationships, especially with older people. Suggest group members share anything about the older people in their lives; write words about the relationships on the board, negative as well as positive. Everyone chooses a word and says it out loud as they walk around the room.

Activities Everyone has a copy of Story Sheet 6, 'Grandmas'.
- Read out the description of the grandma, slowly.
- Invite comments, and explain it was written by a boy of eight years old.
- Read the description again, slowly, and pause after every point the child has made.
- Invite group members to write something about their own grandma or grandpa.
- Decorate the worksheet with colours or stickers.

Sharing Invite group members to read out their descriptions, or show their pictures.

Closure Draw a grandma or grandpa in workbooks; relax with fleeces.

57 Exploring Families

 Children ✓ Teenagers

> **Aims** To encourage group members to express different aspects of family life.

> **Materials** Large whiteboard, coloured markers, fleeces, mats, large drum(s), personal folders and workbooks, crayons and coloured pens.

Warm Up Invite everyone into the circle and encourage feedback. Continue the theme of families, and discuss the way in which it can be difficult to understand some family members. Encourage ideas and give examples, such as, 'Sometimes it is hard to understand why Dad is so cross'. Write ideas on the board. Choose a physical activity to allow any tension to be dispelled.

Activities It is important to reassure group members that they do not have to give examples from their own families; the ideas are simply anything about families that they would like to explore.

- Invite group members to form pairs or threes. (If necessary, choose a warm-up in pairs or threes from the Introduction.)
- Decide on a family situation in which people do not understand each other.
- Show the scene in three freeze-frames (see Introduction).
- Allow the freeze-frames to come to life as the characters move and interact.
- Shake off the roles (see 'de-roling', Introduction).

> **Sharing** In the whole group, talk about the similarities and differences in the scenes.

> **Closure** Using workbooks write or draw some advice for someone who feels troubled; relax with fleeces.

Families: All Sorts & Sizes

58 More about Families

 Children  Teenagers

Aims To encourage group members to verbalise different themes that may run through family life.

Materials Large whiteboard, coloured markers, fleeces, mats, large drum(s), personal folders and workbooks, crayons and coloured pens.

Warm Up Invite everyone into the circle and encourage feedback from previous sessions. Suggest that there may be more to share about families. Perhaps there are ideas that can be drawn from TV soaps, magazines and films? Encourage suggestions and write them on the board. No suggestion should be dismissed, although limits need to be put on extreme violence or violent solutions.

Activities Suggest to the group that it could be useful to explore family situations without any fear that there is only one resolution – there might be several outcomes.

- ⊗ Invite the participants to form groups of three or four, and discuss a possible theme.
- ⊗ Create a tableau to illustrate the theme (see Introduction).
- ⊗ Let the tableau come to life as people are allowed to move.
- ⊗ Then encourage words and sounds.
- ⊗ Come out of the roles by shaking and jumping (see 'de-roling', Introduction).

 This technique of bringing a tableau to life removes a lot of the anxiety from the idea of 'role-play' for children, teenagers and staff. Many people are nervous about role-playing, which often stems from having been 'put on the spot' by inexperienced workshop facilitators. If a group needs lots of encouragement, creating a tableau can be used as a drama game with many different themes, not just the theme of family.

Sharing Discuss the different scenes in the whole group. How close to real life were they?

Closure In workbooks, write one word of advice for a family; relax with fleeces.

 ℗ This page may be photocopied for instructional use only. *101 Activities for Social & Emotional Resilience* © Sue Jennings 2013

59 Family Collage (1)

 Children Teenagers

> **Aims** To provide an opportunity to create a collage on the theme of 'family'.

> **Materials** Large whiteboard, coloured markers, fleeces, mats, large drum(s), personal folders and workbooks, crayons and coloured pens; thick card or paper, glue, scissors, a variety of magazines.

Warm Up Invite everyone into the circle and encourage feedback from previous sessions. Suggest that there are different ways of thinking about families, and that perhaps photographs and words in magazines can be used. The group chooses a physical warm-up.

Activities Everyone has thick paper or card to use as a collage base, as well as magazines, scissors and glue:

- ✪ Suggest that everyone thinks about families, different ages, different relationships.
- ✪ Cut out pictures to create the collage.
- ✪ Cut out words and shapes and phrases.
- ✪ Suggest that everyone first chooses their pictures, then place them on the card, if necessary moving them around before gluing into place.
- ✪ Glue the pictures and words onto the base to form the collage, and colour in any space with pens or crayons.

> **Sharing** In small group, share collages and compare their differences and similarities.

> **Closure** Glue a favourite picture in workbooks; relax with fleeces.

60 Family Collage (2)

☑ Children ☑ Teenagers

Aims To provide an opportunity to create a group collage about 'family'.

Materials Large whiteboard, coloured markers, fleeces, mats, large drum(s), personal folders and workbooks, crayons and coloured pens; large piece of thick card or paper, glue, scissors, a variety of magazines.

Warm Up Invite everyone into the circle and encourage feedback from previous sessions. Suggest that there are different ways of thinking about families, and that perhaps photographs and words in magazines can be used to create a group collage. The group chooses a physical warm-up.

Activities Everyone shares one large piece of thick paper or card, magazines, scissors and glue:

- Suggest that everyone thinks about families, different ages, different relationships, and discusses them in groups.
- Everyone cuts out pictures to create a group collage.
- Everyone cuts out words and shapes and phrases.
- Experiment with fitting the elements together as a group picture.
- Glue the pictures and words onto the base to form the collage, and colour in any space with pens or crayons.

Sharing Discuss in the whole group, and think about the similarities and differences of the images and words on the collage.

Closure Glue another favourite picture in workbooks; relax with fleeces.

Part Seven
School-based Issues: Bullying & Non-Achievement

Activities

Story Sheet

Introduction

School-based issues vary both between individuals and from school to school. There is a range of competencies that deal with bullying, racism and homophobia (Hickson, 2010), and some schools appear to pay lip service to recommendations. However, there are also many schools that have excellent anti-bullying strategies, zero tolerance of violence and a competent pastoral care staff. These are excellent resources, but there may still be difficulties when children and young people lack the skills to actually explain their school issues, or their fear of being mocked or bullied. Keeping quiet may feel more comfortable. This can, of course, give rise to 'silent bullying' (being ignored, stared at, on the receiving end of mouthed threats), cyber bullying, and also being overlooked. The overlooked student will typically sit at the back of a class and literally not be noticed. The techniques in this section address the muddle and confusion that children and teenagers may feel at school, and give examples of how to tell people about problems, and how to ask for help without feeling disadvantaged.

For Activities 66–69, show the group the DVD of *The Wizard of Oz*, and also explain the political influences of the film. (It was made just before the Second World War to emphasise everyone's patriotism and portray women in appropriate roles. No day-dreaming allowed!) This could provoke an interesting debate about manipulation through the media. The role-playing in these activities will help both children and teenagers to develop better communication skills, and allow them to acknowledge their own struggles through the character they are portraying. The story also encourages cooperation and friendship.

61 I Can & I Will!

☑ Children ☑ Teenagers

> **Aims** To support group members who are underachieving in school.

> **Materials** Large whiteboard, coloured markers, fleeces, mats, large drum(s), personal folders and workbooks, crayons and coloured pens.

Warm Up Invite everyone into the circle and encourage feedback from previous sessions. Introduce the word 'pressure', and write people's responses to the word on the board. Use non-competitive games for warm-ups in this section (see Introduction).

Activities Using the drum to lead the rhythm, encourage group members to walk around the room:

- ⊗ Suggest that everyone 'walks tall' to the drum rhythm.
- ⊗ Increase the pace and then slow it down.
- ⊗ As people walk, invite them to call out their names as loudly as possible.
- ⊗ The group walks to the rhythm of the names.
- ⊗ Everyone walks, claps and says their name in rhythm.

> **Sharing** Sit with a partner and share your name and rhythm together.

> **Closure** Sit back to back with a partner and reflect on confidence.

62 The Muddle Stories (1)

☑ Children   ☑ Teenagers

Aims   To encourage group members to express their confusion.

Materials   Large whiteboard, coloured markers, fleeces, mats, large drum(s), personal folders and workbooks, crayons and coloured pens.

Warm Up   Invite everyone into the circle and encourage feedback from previous sessions. Introduce the theme of 'muddles', and the way in which sometimes people do not understand what is being asked of them; invite examples and write them on the board. Everyone scatters around the room. Call out an action and everyone has to do the opposite, for instance: 'Stand up straight', and the participants flop as they stand; 'Run quickly around the room', and everyone walks slowly. Give at least six examples.

Activities   Suggest that everyone makes small groups of three or four:

- ✪ Be aware of the examples on the board and discuss any other 'muddles'.
- ✪ Create a scene to show someone 'not getting it'.
- ✪ Show the scene to the group using a tableau (see Introduction).
- ✪ The other group members can try to guess what the muddle is.
- ✪ Create a second tableau that resolves the misunderstanding in the first.

Sharing   In the whole group, discuss how the muddles were resolved.

Closure   Draw lots of muddled pieces of string or wool in workbooks; relax with fleeces.

63 The Muddle Stories (2)

 ☑ Children ☑ Teenagers

Aims To build self-awareness about confusion.

Materials Large whiteboard, coloured markers, fleeces, mats, large drum(s), personal folders and workbooks, crayons and coloured pens.

Warm Up Invite everyone into the circle, and continue feedback and suggestions about muddles and mistakes. Discuss examples, such as: 'Teacher gets my name wrong'; and 'My PE teacher knows I limp, but forgets.' The group can recognise that adults also make mistakes! Repeat the 'opposites' warm-up in Activity 62.

Activities Invite the group to sit or stand in the circle:

- ✪ Each person chooses an occupation: farmer, plumber, teacher, and so on.
- ✪ Go around the circle; everyone gives their occupation and says what they do; 'I am a plumber, and I mend pipes', and so on.
- ✪ In groups of three, try to remember all the jobs and activities.
- ✪ Share in the whole group how many were remembered.
- ✪ Suggest 'clues' to help us remember, such as imagining the task the person does (visual memory), or remembering a time when we needed that task (contextual memory).

Sharing In the whole group, share things that are difficult to remember, often because the information is confusing.

Closure Draw a ball of wool or string with no muddles in workbooks; relax with fleeces.

64 Clarifications

☑ Children ☑ Teenagers

Aims To develop personal confidence and trust.

Materials Large whiteboard, coloured markers, fleeces, mats, large drum(s), personal folders and workbooks, crayons and coloured pens.

Warm Up Invite everyone into the circle, and encourage feedback from previous sessions. Suggest that the sessions continue with the theme of 'getting it right and getting it wrong'; write any examples on the board. Group members choose their own warm-up.

Activities Create groups of three or four people who have the same first or last letter in their names.

- ✪ Think of a situation where it is easy to get something wrong.
- ✪ Think how to get it right, and what the person trying to get it right might have to ask.
- ✪ Create three sculpts (see Introduction) that illustrate getting it wrong, asking for assistance, then finally getting it right.
- ✪ Show the sculpts to the group.
- ✪ Show the sculpts a second time, adding one word to each sculpt.

Sharing Discuss in the whole group the similarities and differences between the scenes.

Closure Using workbooks, write 'No Muddles' in big, bold letters and colour them in; relax with fleeces.

65 The Muddle Messages

☑ Children   ◯ Teenagers

Aims To support children to express their muddles about school.

Materials Large whiteboard, coloured markers, fleeces, mats, large drum(s), personal folders and workbooks, crayons and coloured pens, A4 paper.

Warm Up Invite everyone into a standing circle. Explain that feedback will be welcomed later in the session. Suggest that everyone flies around the room like an aeroplane, and then imagines they are holding a balloon that is trying to blow away. Finally, with a partner, try to hold down a tent that is about to be carried away by a storm.

Activities Everyone has a piece of A4 paper, crayons and coloured pens:

- ✪ Suggest everyone draws a situation that is difficult to manage at school; these will be kept anonymous.
- ✪ Colour it in and write one word to say what it is.
- ✪ Make a paper aeroplane out of the piece of paper showing the difficult situation (give the group slow, step-by-step instructions if needed).
- ✪ Everyone throws their paper aeroplane across the room.
- ✪ Each person picks up an aeroplane and looks at the picture of the difficult situation.

If there are several pictures that carry the same theme, this may be a common issue in a particular school, such as bullying, or intimidation, or lack of explanations. It needs to be dealt with through school procedures, or even by having a quiet word with a key staff member.

Sharing In the whole group, share the pictures and look at similarities between the difficult situations (no one has to own their picture); give feedback on feelings.

Closure Draw an aeroplane or balloon in workbooks; relax with fleeces.

66 The Wizard of ... (1)

 Children  Teenagers

Aims To encourage participants to acknowledge personal struggles through imaginary characters.

Materials Large whiteboard, coloured markers, fleeces, mats, large drum(s), personal folders and workbooks, crayons and coloured pens; story and DVD of *The Wizard of Oz* (story, words and music are downloadable from the Internet, you can read or show the film to the group if they are not familiar with the story or need to be reminded).

Warm Up Invite everyone into the standing circle. Ask them to run around the room as if they are being blown by strong wind when you call out 'twister'; call out 'shelter', and everyone curls up in a ball; call out 'wicked witch', and everyone holds the hand of their partner and shivers in fear.

Activities Check to see if anyone knows the original story, then read out a brief version of the main points. Suggest that this session concentrates on the Scarecrow who wants a brain and Tin Man who wants a heart:

- ✪ Everyone is Scarecrow and walks in a floppy way (to music).
- ✪ Everyone is Tin Man and walks in a creaking, stiff way (to music or drumbeat).
- ✪ Scarecrow helps Tin Man by oiling his joints.
- ✪ Tin Man helps Scarecrow by pointing out that he can do things himself!
- ✪ In pairs, create sculpts that show meeting, helping and friendship (see Introduction).

Sharing In the whole group, talk about the feelings of the two characters and how they assisted each other.

Closure Draw and colour either Scarecrow or Tin Man in workbooks; relax on fleeces sitting back to back.

67 The Wizard of ... (2)

☑ Children ☑ Teenagers

Aims To further strengthen self-awareness and empowerment.

Materials Large whiteboard, coloured markers, fleeces, mats, large drum(s), personal folders and workbooks, crayons and coloured pens.

Warm Up Invite everyone into a sitting circle and encourage feedback from previous sessions. Did anyone have a favourite character? Introduce Lion who wants courage, and Dorothy who wants to go home; suggest a physical warm-up, during which everyone walks as each of the characters in turn. Then, in pairs, re-enact the scene in which Dorothy tries to persuade Lion to walk on, while he pulls back; change roles.

Activities Share Lion's famous line with the group: while he is talking about his lack of courage, he says, 'I am even frightened of myself!' Discuss what he means.

- ✪ Everyone walks around the room as Lion, jumping at the slightest sound.
- ✪ In pairs, one person is Lion's shadow (following Lion) and the other plays Lion himself; Lion turns around and jumps at his own shadow. Change roles.
- ✪ In pairs, one person is Dorothy who is being kidnapped; the other is Lion who is scared, and then finds courage to rescue her with a loud roar! Change roles.
- ✪ Create sculpts of Dorothy being kidnapped, Lion scared, and Lion being brave.
- ✪ Share with group, encouraging everyone to portray their characters 'larger than life'.

Sharing In the whole group, share feelings about being the characters; link to the previous session and consider that Scarecrow, Tin Man, Lion and Dorothy can work together.

Closure Draw and colour Lion or Dorothy in workbooks; relax on fleeces, back to back with a partner.

68 The Wizard of ... (3)

 Children  Teenagers

Aims To build confidence and coping skills through cultivating an active imagination.

Materials Large whiteboard, coloured markers, fleeces, mats, large drum(s), personal folders and workbooks, crayons and coloured pens.

Warm Up Invite everyone into the standing circle. Suggest that the group can take the Wizard story further. As everyone runs around the room, being blown by the fierce winds of the twister, they can think about the Wizard who turns out to be a fake, the Good Witch and the Wicked Witch, and the power of the red shoes. Call out 'Freeze!' and the group freeze as if they are the Wicked Witch. The group runs again; then call out 'Freeze!' and the group freeze as if they are the Good Witch. How might the voices of the two witches be different?

Activities Each person works with a partner to develop small scenes or sculpts:

- ✪ One partner is the Wizard who talks about achievements that are not real; the other listens, then challenges, and the Wizard has to try to convince them again.
- ✪ The Wizard makes a promise to the partner and then rushes off before fulfilling it.
- ✪ The Good Witch and the Bad Witch have an argument about who should have the red shoes.
- ✪ Exaggerate the characters, gestures and voices.
- ✪ Share a favourite scene or sculpt using the whole group.

Sharing Discuss in the whole group individual likes and dislikes; talk about the entire story of the Wizard and how it fits together.

Closure Using workbooks, write or draw a favourite character from the story; relax on fleeces with a partner, back to back.

69 The Wizard of ... (4)

✓ Children ✓ Teenagers

> **Aims** To further build the use of an active imagination that enhances coping skills.

> **Materials** Large whiteboard, coloured markers, fleeces, mats, large drum(s), personal folders and workbooks, crayons and coloured pens; hats, caps, scarves, wands, card for making props, sticky tape.

Warm Up Invite everyone into the standing circle and welcome brief feedback from previous Wizard sessions. Suggest that everyone performs an everyday activity that would be normal for the first characters in the story: the farm workers, the nasty teacher, Dorothy, or Aunt Em. When the drum beats, the twister storm blows them all to a new land and they change into a new character. After a little role-playing as their new character, everyone can be blown back again.

Activities Build directly on the warm-up and introduce the idea of changes: some people may change without realising it after a sudden shock, or they may choose to change – others go back to behaving exactly as they always have!

- ✪ Small groups of four or five people choose a favourite scene from the story.
- ✪ Allow time for exploration of the way in which they might show the scene.
- ✪ Encourage participants to create their own ideas, rather than slavishly following the film.
- ✪ Give permission for the use of words or no words, and simple props.
- ✪ Share scenes in whole group with music, if needed.

> **Sharing** Encourage positive feedback on the scenes and stories; ensure de-roling at the end of the session (see Introduction).

> **Closure** Using workbooks, write or draw your favourite experience in the story; relax with fleeces.

School-based Issues: Bullying & Non-Achievement

70 Friends who are Different

☑ Children ◯ Teenagers

Aims To assist younger children in understanding their differences and sharing.

Materials Large whiteboard, coloured markers, fleeces, mats, large drum(s), personal folders and workbooks, crayons and coloured pens; Story Sheet 7.

Warm Up Invite everyone into the circle and suggest it is time for animals: call out animal names and everyone walks or crawls as that animal; then everyone chooses a different animal and moves towards the other animals in the room and away from them. Read Story Sheet 7, 'The Four Friends', to the group and invite comment. The poem involves an elephant that trumpets very loudly, a lion that roars, a goat with a compass, and a snail that can travel the length of a brick.

Activities Continue the theme of 'The Four Friends':

- ✪ Suggest that everyone moves and makes sounds as the elephant, then the lion, then the goat, and then the snail.
- ✪ In pairs, choose two characters and let them communicate with each other.
- ✪ In groups of four, everyone takes it in turn to be each of the animals.
- ✪ Think of a scene where the animals need the goat's compass, the concentration of the snail and the noise of the large animals.
- ✪ The scenes can be sculpted, drawn or enacted.

Sharing In the whole group, discuss the four friends and how they help each other.

Closure Draw one of the animals in workbooks; relax with fleeces.

Part Eight
Decision-Making & Problem Solving

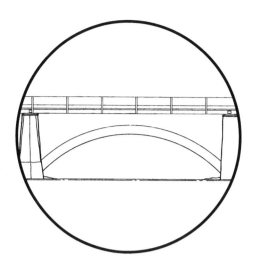

Activities

Worksheets

Introduction

Some decision-making has already been built into the programme of activities: individuals and groups have to make choices about exercises and warm ups, or are asked to choose one character rather than another. The drama session not only promotes creativity, it also provides opportunities for lots of social-skills learning, communication and problem solving. Drama is the best means of enabling the less resilient child to achieve confidence, self-control and choice management.

Drama is often associated with scary confrontation, or perceived as airy-fairy and not relevant to mainstream education. However, research has demonstrated that children and teenagers who are engaged in active learning both retain and understand information and concepts better than those who have received information in a passive way.

As participants build up their resilience, thus decreasing their neediness, over-reactive behaviour and lack of control, it will be noticed that their life skills and social skills continue to increase.

71 Choices about Me (1)

☑ Children ☑ Teenagers

> **Aims** To develop more confident decision-making.

> **Materials** Large whiteboard, coloured markers, fleeces, mats, large drum(s), personal folders and workbooks, crayons and coloured pens, A4 paper.

Warm Up Invite everyone into the circle and encourage participants to share how they would like to increase their self-confidence. Write key words on the board. Many people feel that other people make decisions for them, rather than feeling that they can choose for themselves. All the warm-ups in this section will be chosen by group members, after consultation with the whole group (WGC/ICh, or Whole Group Consultation, Individual Choice).

Activities Bring everyone into a standing circle and develop the following drama games for choices:

- ✪ Everyone chooses a favourite colour and then tries to persuade the others to choose their colour, but each person should stick to their original choice.

- ✪ Everyone chooses a favourite band or singer, and the others try to persuade them to change their minds, without success.

- ✪ Suggest that everyone makes a silly choice of TV programme, and then gives a speech to say how wonderful the programme is!

- ✪ On A4 paper, everyone writes or draws a page of choices for their lives. Under each one write 'this is my choice'.

- ✪ Draw a big picture of the most important choice.

> **Sharing** Work in pairs with someone who will disagree with your choice. Discuss in a friendly way the choices of both partners.

> **Closure** Using workbooks, draw or write the most important choice; relax with fleeces.

Decision-Making & Problem Solving

72 Choices about Me (2)

 Children Teenagers

Decision-Making & Problem Solving

Aims To continue personal decision-making.

Materials Large whiteboard, coloured markers, fleeces, mats, large drum(s), personal folders and workbooks, crayons and coloured pens.

Warm Up Invite everyone into the circle, and encourage feedback from previous sessions. Continue the idea of personal choice rather than group pressure. Remind people that often people think choices are either/or, when in reality there are shades of grey! WGC/ICh. Group members may need help with the initial group consultation, but soon they will be on a roll!

Activities Use a scattering and running around the room exercise if the group needs more physical warm-up.

- ✪ Create pairs with someone with different views about something.
- ✪ Choose an activity that is simple and silly.
- ✪ Decide on serious reasons for doing a silly activity.
- ✪ Show the activity to the other members of the group, who try to persuade the pair it is silly.
- ✪ Work together to hang onto your own reasons for doing the activity.

Sharing Discuss with a partner any changes in feelings of self-confidence.

Closure Tell partners about the symbol that gives you confidence; relax with fleeces.

---

73 Choices about Me (3)

☑ Children ☑ Teenagers

Aims To continue personal decision-making.

Materials Large whiteboard, coloured markers, fleeces, mats, large drum(s), personal folders and workbooks, crayons and coloured pens; paints, paint brushes, glue, scissors and lots of recycled materials (such as cardboard, wool, foil, scraps of fabric, old wrapping paper and ribbons).

Warm Up Invite everyone into a sitting circle, and encourage feedback from previous sessions. Write key words on the board. WGC/ICh.

Activities Reassure older groups that this is not an infant class with empty sweet wrappers! It is based on the principle of reusing materials *and* exercising the imagination.

- ✪ Choose a partner and decide on a model to build from the scraps and recycled materials.
- ✪ The choice of model is completely free.
- ✪ Paint or colour any parts if needed.
- ✪ Choose a name for model or invention.
- ✪ Show your models to the other groups.

Sharing In the whole group, discuss the transformation from rubbish to model.

Closure Draw models in workbooks; relax with fleeces.

Decision-Making & Problem Solving

74 Recycling Myself!

 Children  Teenagers

Aims To encourage participants to change their perceptions of themselves.

Materials Large whiteboard, coloured markers, fleeces, mats, large drum(s), personal folders and workbooks, crayons and coloured pens; Worksheet 20.

Warm Up Invite everyone into the circle and encourage feedback from previous sessions. Develop a discussion about self-image and how people see themselves. WCG/ICh.

Activities Each person has Worksheet 20, 'I Can Recycle Myself! (1)', as well as crayons and coloured pens:

- ✪ Explain that the worksheet shows a pile of rubbish.
- ✪ Suggest that everyone changes the rubbish into a positive picture by colouring.
- ✪ New objects can be added, and existing objects can be changed.
- ✪ Create a frame for the picture.
- ✪ Give the picture a name.

Sharing Create an art gallery displaying all the pictures, and look at the different ways the rubbish has been transformed into something positive.

Closure Draw a robot made of rubbish in workbooks; relax with fleeces.

75 Changing How I See Myself

☑ Children ☑ Teenagers

Aims Encouraging participants to 'change the labels' and to let go of negative self-image.

Materials Large whiteboard, coloured markers, fleeces, mats, large drum(s), personal folders and workbooks, crayons and coloured pens; Worksheet 21.

Warm Up Invite everyone into the circle and encourage feedback from previous sessions. Continue the discussion of self-perception and write any ideas on board. WGC/ICh.

Activities Everyone has Worksheet 21, 'I Can Recycle Myself' (2), as well as crayons and coloured pens:

- ✪ Explain that everyone has a choice to 'let go' of things that are unhelpful.
- ✪ Look at the words on the worksheet and colour in any that you want to put in the bin.
- ✪ Write down and let go of more words or drawings that are personal to you.
- ✪ Think about the opposite, positive words, and write them in the boxes at the bottom of the worksheet to replace the negative words.
- ✪ Create a coloured border of positive words and pictures.

Sharing With a partner, tell them what is going in the bin, and say the positive words together – you could even create a chant that might develop into a group chant of positive words.

Closure Draw and colour a positive word in workbooks; relax with fleeces.

Decision-Making & Problem Solving

76 Positive Chant

 Children  Teenagers

> **Aims** To encourage participants to embody positive qualities through the body and voice.

> **Materials** Large whiteboard, coloured markers, fleeces, mats, large drum(s), personal folders and workbooks, crayons and coloured pens.

Warm Up Invite everyone into a circle and encourage feedback from previous sessions. Write any key words on the board. Continue with the theme of positive qualities and write more positive words on the board. WGC/ICh.

Activities Bring everyone into a standing circle and explain the following exercise:

- ✪ Encourage everyone to choose one particular positive word.
- ✪ They say their word under their breath at first, then louder, then quieter.
- ✪ Choose a partner and put the two words together as a chant.
- ✪ Use the chant to develop a movement sequence on the spot.
- ✪ Continue the movement chant around the room, and repeat it on the spot.

> **Sharing** Every pair shows their movement chant to the group.

> **Closure** Write your most important positive word in workbooks; relax with fleeces.

  ⓟ This page may be photocopied for instructional use only. *101 Activities for Social & Emotional Resilience* © Sue Jennings 2013

77 My Positive Profile

✓ Children   ✓ Teenagers

Aims   To develop a strong self-image.

Materials   Large whiteboard, coloured markers, fleeces, mats, large drum(s), personal folders and workbooks, crayons and coloured pens; magazines and newspaper supplements, glue, scissors, A4 paper.

Warm Up   Invite everyone into the circle and encourage feedback from previous sessions. Continue acknowledging positive personal qualities and write ideas on the board. WGC/ICh.

Activities   Everyone has magazines, newspaper supplements, scissors, glue, A4 paper:

- ✪ Cut out positive words that describe personal qualities.
- ✪ Create a collage of words.
- ✪ Link the words with coloured lines.
- ✪ Frame the collages with coloured symbols.
- ✪ Decide on a title for the picture.

Sharing   Work in pairs to compare collage pictures and contrast different words.

Closure   Write the most important positive word in workbooks; relax with fleeces.

Decision-Making & Problem Solving

78 Let Bygones be Bygones

 Children Teenagers

Aims To encourage participants not to hold on to hurts and jealousies.

Materials Large whiteboard, coloured markers, fleeces, mats, large drum(s), personal folders and workbooks, crayons and coloured pens; Worksheet 22.

Warm Up Invite everyone into the circle and encourage feedback from previous sessions. Suggest that sometimes people hold on to things from the past, and they can feel anxious or tense or hurt about those. Invite examples and write them on the board. WGC/ICh.

Activities Everyone has Worksheet 22, 'Why Not Let Bygones be Bygones?', as well as crayons and coloured pens;

- ✪ Invite everyone to close their eyes and think of something that happened to them in the past that was mean or unkind.
- ✪ Remember the words of Nelson Mandela, one of the most famous and forgiving people in the world: 'Let bygones be bygones'.
- ✪ Give the memory a shape and a colour and one word; then draw these on the worksheet or color in the picture.
- ✪ Draw a positive image, feeling or symbol and colour it.
- ✪ Everyone says to themselves, 'Let bygones be bygones'.

Sharing With the whole group, discuss how hard it is to let go of things that are felt to be unfair, mean or spiteful. Does it help us to hold on to them?

Closure Write a positive word in workbooks; relax with fleeces.

Decision-Making & Problem Solving

79 Deciding to Let Go

☑ Children ☑ Teenagers

Aims To let go of past hurts through body work.

Materials Large whiteboard, coloured markers, fleeces, mats, large drum(s), personal folders and workbooks, crayons and coloured pens; relaxing music.

Warm Up Invite everyone into the circle and encourage feedback from the previous session about personal hurts. Suggest that sometimes we hold on to these hurts physically, leading to headaches, tummy cramps, stiff jaws, and so. Write suggestions on the board. WGC/ICh. Invite the group to choose two warm-ups.

Activities Everyone finds a space on the floor to lie down on their mat or fleece:

❂ Each person wriggles around until they feel comfortable; play relaxing music in background.

❂ Breathe slowly in through the nose and out through the mouth, several times.

❂ Think of any aches and pains that are caused by tension.

❂ Imagine lying in a warm place where everything is relaxed, and continue deep breathing; just listen to the music for a few minutes.

❂ Turn on to your side, curl up tight, relax and stretch.

Sharing Stand up in the whole group, stretch and sit back to back with a partner, continue to relax.

Closure Continue to listen to music; relax with fleeces.

Decision-Making & Problem Solving

80 # The New Road & The Old Road

 Children Teenagers

Aims To support participants in making decisions about change.

Materials Large whiteboard, coloured markers, fleeces, mats, large drum(s), personal folders and workbooks, crayons and coloured pens; Worksheet 23.

Warm Up Invite everyone into the circle and encourage feedback from previous sessions. Introduce the idea of making choices about new directions, and write any words and ideas on the board. WGC/ICh.

Activities Everyone has Worksheet 23, 'Choosing the Road', as well as coloured pens and crayons:

- ✪ Continue the discussion of new roads and paths ahead.
- ✪ How does each person's current road look? Straight? Twisted? Muddled? Cluttered? Miserable? Lonely?
- ✪ Colour in the current road on worksheets and write on it any important words.
- ✪ Think about how a new road could look. Will it be clear? Will there be new directions? Friends? Activities? Colour in the new road and write any important words.

Sharing Discuss in the whole group how roads vary with individuals.

Closure Using workbooks, write or draw the most important thing on the new road; relax with fleeces.

Part Nine
Theatre of Resilience: Integrating New Experiences

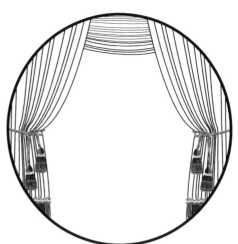

Activities

Worksheets

Introduction

For many people the word 'theatre' means a seasonal entertainment or the local operatic group, or even something that engenders fear and anxiety! Memories of being made to 'perform' at school often leave their mark. And after all hasn't TV replaced the need for theatre?

However, if we observe the play of young children, it can be seen that they master their skills through performing them; they overcome fears by 'acting them out' with puppets, stories or the doll's house. Play, dramatic play and drama continue to be an important means of developing and practising life and social skills, as well as encouraging the creative process of the right hemisphere of the brain. Dramatic play and performance are crucial for neurological development, and for improving the likelihood of behavioural change and increased resilience.

This next section is a culmination of the previous sections that have created the building blocks for resilient growth.

81 One Step at a Time (1)

☑ Children ☑ Teenagers

Aims To build up internal strengths for change.

Materials Large whiteboard, coloured markers, fleeces, mats, large drum(s), personal folders and workbooks, crayons and coloured pens; lively music.

Warm Up Invite everyone into the circle. Encourage discussion of life changes, and how easy it is to get stuck in old ways; write themes on the board. WGC/ICh.

Activities Everyone scatters around the room and freezes; play rhythmic music:

- ☸ Walk in straight lines, turning at the end of the room or in the corners.
- ☸ Walk in curves, weaving in and out, not touching anyone else.
- ☸ Half of the group walk in straight lines, half in curves, in and out with no touching; then change over.
- ☸ Create a game where half the group make a line across the room and decide on a password.
- ☸ The other half have to guess the password, or try to negotiate a way across the line in another way.

Sharing Each person chooses a partner from the other group. Hold hands and pull each other across the room; everyone tries to stand their ground.

Closure Draw an open door or gate in workbooks; relax with fleeces.

Theatre of Resilience: Integrating New Experiences

82 One Step at a Time (2)

☑ Children ◯ Teenagers

Aims To support participants in naming a new step for their lives.

Materials Large whiteboard, coloured markers, fleeces, mats, large drum(s), personal folders and workbooks, crayons and coloured pens; Worksheet 24.

Warm Up Invite everyone into the circle and encourage feedback about changes that people feel have happened to them since being in the group; write important words on the board. Introduce the idea of role-play and rehearsal. Encourage both vocal and physical warm-up when group members choose WGC/ICh.

Activities Everyone has Worksheet 24, 'Take One Step at a Time', as well as crayons and coloured pens:

✪ Introduce the theme of taking one small step forward; everyone thinks about a small step they might take.

✪ Use the worksheet to draw your idea and write about that step.

✪ Is more than one step possible? Think about the possibilities.

✪ Write and colour what these remaining steps might be.

✪ Write down some words to make a statement about taking steps forward.

Sharing Encourage group members to share their worksheet with their partner, and to compare differences. Perhaps partners can suggest other small steps to each other?

Closure Using workbooks, draw and colour a favourite shoe with which to make a step; relax with fleeces.

Theatre of Resilience: Integrating New Experiences

83 One Step at a Time (3)

☑ Children   ☑ Teenagers

> **Aims** To encourage group members to bring a sense of fun to change and performance.

> **Materials** Large whiteboard, coloured markers, fleeces, mats, large drum(s), personal folders and workbooks, crayons and coloured pens; fashion magazines of all sorts, scissors, glue, A3 paper or card.

Warm Up Invite everyone into the circle and encourage feedback about previous sessions. Remind group members that this work can be fun. WGC/ICh, especially warm-ups that emphasise feet!

Activities In small groups, everyone has one piece of A3 paper, magazines, scissors, glue and coloured pens:

- ✪ Each group creates a collage of different footwear – male and female.
- ✪ Cut out pictures of boots, shoes, sandals, slippers, beach shoes, climbing boots, fantasy shoes, or magic shoes.
- ✪ Use coloured pens to link all the footwear on the collage.
- ✪ Draw additional shoes if there are too few choices.
- ✪ Remember to include cartoon shoes.

> **Sharing** With a partner, discuss which shoe would be most help in taking a first step forward.

> **Closure** Draw a favourite shoe in workbooks; relax with fleeces.

84 One Step at a Time (4)

 Children  Teenagers

Aims To reinforce the first step that everyone wishes to take.

Materials Large whiteboard, coloured markers, fleeces, mats, large drum(s), personal folders and workbooks, crayons and coloured pens; shoe collages from previous session.

Warm Up Invite everyone into the circle and encourage feedback from previous sessions; continue the theme of first steps. WGC/ICh.

Activities Encourage everyone to think about sayings to do with feet or foot activity, for example: 'best foot forward', 'wrong-footed', 'these boots were made for walking', and so on.

- ✪ In groups of two to three, choose a phrase and create a sculpt (freeze-frame); show it to group.
- ✪ Bring the sculpt to life and see what happens (use words or movement).
- ✪ Experiment with the saying in several different ways.
- ✪ Choose one version to develop, and make a scene.
- ✪ Share all the scenes with the whole group.

Sharing In the whole group, discuss how the scenes changed through the improvisation.

Closure Draw a cartoon of the saying in workbooks; relax with fleeces.

85 One Step at a Time (5)

 Children  Teenagers

> **Aims** To continue the reinforcement of everyone's first step.

> **Materials** Large whiteboard, coloured markers, fleeces, mats, large drum(s), personal folders and workbooks, crayons and coloured pens; a variety of hats and caps.

Warm Up Invite everyone into the circle and welcome feedback, both about previous sessions and also about how people are feeling right now. Remind everyone of the general theme of taking one step at a time; encourage the group to give examples from their own lives, and write ideas on the board. WGC/ICh.

Activities Play some warm-up games to get the group really mixed (e.g., Warm-ups 3, 14 or 19); then add the hats, so that people have to change hats as they change groups (e.g., Warm-up 11). Finish by forming into groups of three:

- ✪ Discuss a theme for a scene about 'one step forward'. It can be based on a personal situation, an amalgam of the group members' experience, or something completely new.
- ✪ Start by creating a sculpt of the scene.
- ✪ Elaborate the sculpt into a drama.
- ✪ Keep rehearsing the drama and explore different approaches.

> **Sharing** Show the scenes to the whole group and give positive feedback.

> **Closure** Using workbooks, draw and colour a favourite character from the drama; relax with fleeces.

Theatre of Resilience: Integrating New Experiences

86 Festival of Stories (1)

 Children  Teenagers

> **Aims** To enable participants to feel more confident in performance.

> **Materials** Large whiteboard, coloured markers, fleeces, mats, large drum(s), personal folders and workbooks, crayons and coloured pens; lots of hats and caps, ideas of traditional stories and sayings.

Warm Up Invite everyone into the circle and share feedback from previous session; encourage everyone to think of stories and sayings from their own culture or family. WGC/ICh.

Activities Use warm-up number games to form people into groups of three or four, and tell everyone to be prepared for storytelling.

- ✪ Everyone shares a story or a saying (however brief) with their small group.
- ✪ Who told the story originally? A parent? Grandparent?
- ✪ Choose one story to share with the whole group.
- ✪ Decide on a way to tell the story as a performance, with costumes and props.
- ✪ Perform the story to the whole group.

> **Sharing** Share thoughts and observations in the whole group, and encourage feedback about new things that have been understood.

> **Closure** Draw a symbol from someone else's story in workbooks; relax with fleeces.

87 Festival of Stories (2)

 Children Teenagers

Aims To promote sharing across cultures and encourage performance skills.

Materials Large whiteboard, coloured markers, fleeces, mats, large drum(s), personal folders and workbooks, crayons and coloured pens; hats, caps, large pieces of fabric, belts, additional drums, A3 paper, A2 paper or card.

Warm Up Invite everyone into the circle and encourage feedback from previous sessions; suggest the group continues to think about traditions and stories from different cultures and families. WGC/ICh.

Activities Announce to the group that there is to be a 'Festival of Stories and Drama from Different Cultures', and that it will be explored over three sessions and will include one performance. Discuss whether or not other people could be invited to watch.

- ✪ In small groups (carried over from the previous session), decide on the story or drama to perform; this could be a continuation of the scene from Activity 86 or a new choice.
- ✪ Create a poster together in the small groups to advertise the event.
- ✪ Include the title, characters, as well as any props that are important to the drama, and colour the poster with the right kind of colours.
- ✪ Encourage the whole group to create one large, joint poster with everyone contributing.
- ✪ Put all the posters up on the wall; take some time for everyone to look and comment.

Sharing In the whole group give comments and encouragement.

Closure Draw an image from the poster in workbooks; relax with fleeces.

Theatre of Resilience: Integrating New Experiences

88 Festival of Stories (3)

☑ Children ☑ Teenagers

Aims To encourage group members to take pride in their own culture.

Materials Large whiteboard, coloured markers, fleeces, mats, large drum(s), personal folders and workbooks, crayons and coloured pens; music for the different scenes or stories, props, fabric.

Warm Up Invite everyone into the circle and suggest only brief feedback as there is a show to prepare! Suggest leader-led warm-ups to dispel anxiety, and focus everyone on the task in hand.

Activities It is important to reassure group members that it this not a competition; it is a sharing of different dramas and stories. The rules of performance (whether there is an outside audience or not) are formal: punctual start times, remaining attentive and supporting each other.

- Create a performance area using chairs and fabric to show the edge of the stage.
- Choose a narrator to introduce the scenes.
- Each group portrays their story or scene; the others help with staging.
- Everyone comes together at the end to take a bow.
- Shake off the roles as group members 'de-role'.

Sharing If there is an outside audience, invite questions from audience members; otherwise, pack up the props and costumes, and sit in a circle for discussion.

Closure Draw a picture that represents the whole festival in workbooks; relax with fleeces.

89 Festival of Stories (4)

> **Aims** To encourage group members to verbalise their own opinions and develop the skills of positive criticism.

> **Materials** Large whiteboard, coloured markers, fleeces, mats, large drum(s), personal folders and workbooks, crayons and coloured pens.

Warm Up Invite everyone into the circle and encourage feedback from previous sessions; suggest group members give individual comments about the performances. WGC/ICh.

Activities Suggest to the group that they could be newspaper critics who have opinions, and that they can 'have their say' about the Festival.

- ✪ Everyone forms smaller groups of three who will comment together.
- ✪ Discuss one of the scenes and write down key words.
- ✪ Write or draw the comments and encourage positive ways of communication, even if some of the points are critical.
- ✪ Share the 'crits' with the other groups.
- ✪ Try to find a balance between the different comments.

> **Sharing** Discuss the different scenes and comments in the whole group.

> **Closure** Write some positive words about the scenes in workbooks; relax with fleeces.

Theatre of Resilience: Integrating New Experiences

90 What Would Make a Difference?

 Children   Teenagers

Aims To provide opportunities for group members to acknowledge continuing needs.

Materials Large whiteboard, coloured markers, fleeces, mats, large drum(s), personal folders and workbooks, crayons and coloured pens; Worksheet 25.

Warm Up Invite everyone into the circle and encourage feedback from previous sessions. Remind everyone that this is the final session of this type, and now is the time to acknowledge issues that have not been addressed previously. WGC/ICh.

Activities Everyone has Worksheet 25, 'What Would Make a Difference?', as well as crayons and coloured pens.

- ✪ Think about all the sessions that have been held and the things that are helpful for you now.
- ✪ Think about things that could be helpful in the future.
- ✪ What would make a difference now?
- ✪ Using the worksheet, colour and write people or things or thoughts.
- ✪ Colour a border on the worksheet.

Sharing Discuss in the whole group whether any needs can be let go, and how other needs can be realised.

Closure Write final positive words in workbooks; relax with fleeces.

  This page may be photocopied for instructional use only. *101 Activities for Social & Emotional Resilience* © Sue Jennings 2013

Part Ten
The Great Outdoors: Contact with Nature

Activities

Worksheets

Introduction

There was a time, before Health and Safety Rules, when working in nature was a part of the regular curriculum in many schools. There would be outings to adventure parks, farms, walks in woods and forests, and picnics at the seaside or on a riverbank. Extra time would be allowed for playing in the snow, rather than schools closing down. It is as if these days everyone needs to be protected from nature, rather than being able to live in its midst. It seems a paradox that people are protected *from* nature, rather than realising that nature itself requires protection!

Every school and therapeutic centre has its own rules and safety considerations, so the techniques in this section will be governed by what is allowed in each location. Some of the suggestions may need to be adapted, or special permission sought, bearing in mind that insurance premiums escalate if activities are deemed to be dangerous.

Nevertheless, working with and in nature is very important for developing resilience. Nature itself needs a different form of coping, and not all children and young people adapt spontaneously. If an individual or group have suffered a traumatic experience in nature, such as flood, lightning, mudslide, for example, then a return to nature could be a scary experience. This needs to be checked out in advance.

At the end of a resilience programme such as this one, it is useful to consider a summer camp, overnight stays in wooded or wild areas, and especially a visit to the Eden Project (www.edenproject.com) if possible.

Some of the previous exercises, such as the worksheets with leaf people, the drumming techniques and the Worry Tree story, can also be adapted for use in this section.

91 Nature Story (1)

☑ Children ☑ Teenagers

Aims   To introduce participants to the idea of working with nature and to build up their confidence.

Materials   Large whiteboard, coloured markers (only if working indoors); fleeces, mats, large drum(s), personal folders and workbooks, crayons and coloured pens.

Warm Up   Invite everyone into an outdoor circle (if possible) and talk about how working with nature can build up personal and group strengths. If the group needs energising, suggest a game of tag or chase.

Activities   Share with the group that the various exercises can be done outside or be adapted to indoors:

- ✪ Everyone scatters and brings back to the group one natural object they have found: leaves, twigs, acorns, oak apples, blossom, and so on (everything should be picked up off the ground, with nothing pulled from trees or bushes, or out of the earth).
- ✪ In groups of three, use the objects to create a story about nature.
- ✪ Discuss how the story could be told to the group and keep their attention; maybe there is more than one style of storytelling?
- ✪ Tell the stories to the whole group, remembering the varied use of voice and gestures.
- ✪ Try telling another group's story and see if it changes when told by others.

Sharing   Discuss the stories in the whole group and think about similarities and differences.

Closure   Draw one of the natural objects in workbooks; relax with fleeces.

The Great Outdoors: Contact with Nature

92 Nature Story (2)

 ✓ Children ⭘ Teenagers

Aims To encourage participants to connect with nature themes.

Materials Large whiteboard, coloured markers (if working indoors); fleeces, mats, large drum(s), personal folders and workbooks, crayons and coloured pens; a pile of different, fresh leaves.

Warm Up Invite everyone into the circle and welcome feedback from the previous session. Encourage group members to talk about their own experiences in the natural world. Play a game of hide and seek, especially if there are trees nearby.

Activities Encourage everyone to look for leaves outdoors or use the leaves provided in the group room (you could also use the leaf people from Worksheet 4, 'I Feel Lost').

⊗ Compare the different shapes, colours, veins and textures.

⊗ Notice the differences and similarities in leaves from the same tree.

⊗ Identify the trees that the leaves have come from.

⊗ Choose a leaf to draw around and colour.

⊗ Create a short story about the leaf providing shelter for a small animal or insect.

Sharing Discuss in the whole group the importance of all leaves and all people.

Closure Draw the insect or small animal in workbooks; relax with fleeces.

93 Bringing Nature Inside (1)

☑ Children ☑ Teenagers

| **Aims** | To encourage group members to explore the world outside. |

| **Materials** | Large whiteboard, coloured markers, fleeces, mats, large drum(s), personal folders and workbooks, crayons and coloured pens; collection of small stones, twigs, bark, acorns, shells and so on; several trays of sand, one between three people (large circular trays for standing beneath plant pots are ideal). |

Warm Up   Invite everyone into the group and encourage feedback about previous sessions. Share the idea that there are stories about nature, but also that nature can help us to tell our own stories. Introduce the idea of societies where 'sand art' tells the story of the tribe. WGC/ICh.

Activities   Form groups of three to each sand tray, with a selection of natural objects.

- ✪ Remind group members that pictures can tell stories.
- ✪ Each group makes its own picture with the natural objects.
- ✪ Encourage collaboration and working together.
- ✪ Once the picture is complete, share ideas about the story it might tell.
- ✪ Agree a story that can be told to the group.

| **Sharing** | Each group tells their story to the others, and shows their sand picture. Then the groups carefully dismantle their own pictures (photos could be taken before the pictures are taken apart). |

| **Closure** | Draw the sand picture in workbooks; relax with fleeces. |

94 # Bringing Nature Inside (2)

 Children Teenagers

Aims To encourage participants to collaborate through the medium of nature.

Materials Large whiteboard, coloured markers, fleeces, mats, large drum(s), personal folders and workbooks, crayons and coloured pens; A3 sheets of paper, nature pictures from a variety of magazines (such as animals, landscapes, and so on), white glue, scissors.

Warm Up Invite everyone into the group and encourage feedback. Continue the theme of nature and our different responses to it. WGC/ICh.

Activities Reintroduce the idea of nature and stories. The group forms into pairs and each pair has a sheet of A3 paper, crayons, coloured pens, large paper, white glue and scissors.

- ✪ Allow time for everyone to look at each magazine picture.
- ✪ Each pair chooses one nature picture that suggests a story.
- ✪ Discuss the landscape and the creatures, expanding the picture with your own ideas and stories.
- ✪ Create a joint collage, combining the nature picture and your own drawings.
- ✪ Colour in any gaps between the drawings and the photos.

Sharing Show the collages to whole group and share how ideas can be expanded and developed.

Closure Draw something from the collage in workbooks; relax with fleeces.

95 Bringing Nature Inside (3)

☑ Children ☑ Teenagers

> **Aims** To assist children and teenagers to be aware of connections between themselves and nature.

> **Materials** Large whiteboard, coloured markers, fleeces, mats, large drum(s), personal folders and workbooks, crayons and coloured pens.

Warm Up Invite everyone into the circle and encourage feedback, both about previous sessions and also about how people are feeling right now. Introduce the idea of the weather and nature being a helpful way to talk about feelings. Write examples on the board, for example: 'I feel like a volcano', or 'There's a storm brewing'. Create warm-ups based on the weather and the behaviour of the elements: huge waves, hurricanes, gentle breezes, and so on.

Activities This exercise needs plenty of space for people to move around:

- ⊗ Working in groups of three or four, explore different movements to express weather and nature (taking the lead from the warm-up).
- ⊗ Encourage contrasts and extremes: drops of rain, followed by a huge thunderstorm (prompt the action and sounds from the side if necessary).
- ⊗ Drums can also be used to provide sounds and rhythms.
- ⊗ In small groups put a sequence together that has a beginning and an end – a 'movement' landscape.
- ⊗ The whole group creates a continuous landscape from the several group scenes, one scene following another.

> **Sharing** Discuss in the whole group any ideas and thoughts about the nature activities.

> **Closure** Using workbooks, draw and colour a picture of the movement landscape; relax with fleeces.

96 The Biggest Sand Tray (1)

 Children   Teenagers

Aims To encourage participants to work in nature, developing respect for the environment and themselves.

Materials Drums and access to a large beach with sand, or a field with a riverbank, or a woodland area (if possible, with water).

Warm Up Invite everyone into the circle and share feedback from previous session. Make sure the ground rules are heard and understood, including all health and safety issues. Everyone takes it in turn to create a physical warm-up, including running, jumping and circle games. Establish a signal for the moment when everyone has to stand still and listen.

Activities Everyone works with a partner within an agreed area, after initial exploration:

- ✪ The whole group walks through the space to understand its limits; if necessary, put flags on sticks to show the boundaries.
- ✪ Create personal 'pair space' with a circle of stones or other natural markers.
- ✪ Working with a partner, choose various objects and bring them to your space.
- ✪ Use the objects to make a picture inside the circle.
- ✪ Decide if the picture tells a story.

Sharing Everyone visits everyone else's picture and shares comments and any stories.

Closure Sit back to back with your partner and listen to any sounds in the environment.

97 The Biggest Sand Tray (2)

✓ Children ✓ Teenagers

> **Aims** To fine-tune the senses to sounds and textures in nature.

> **Materials** Drums and access to a large beach with sand, or a field with a riverbank, or a woodland area (if possible, with water).

Warm Up   Invite everyone into the circle and encourage feedback from previous session. Share anything new that the group has experienced through working in nature. Make sure the ground rules are heard and understood, including all health and safety issues. Everyone takes it in turns to create a physical warm-up, including running, jumping and circle games. Establish a signal for the moment when everyone has to stand still and listen.

Activities   Everyone sits in threes, near enough to be able to hear instructions:

- ✪ Encourage everyone to close their eyes, and to breathe deeply and slowly for a few minutes.
- ✪ Focus on the sounds that can be heard around you in nature.
- ✪ Focus on the sounds of your own body, such as heartbeat and breathing.
- ✪ Open the eyes and, in small groups, share the different sounds that have been heard.
- ✪ Using voice and rhythms, create a 'sound' picture.

> **Sharing** Everyone shares sound pictures and puts them together in a sequence.

> **Closure** Relax in a sitting or lying position and listen to sounds from nature.

98 # If I Were a Tree ...

☑ Children ☑ Teenagers

| **Aims** | To encourage group members to explore metaphors through tree emblems. |

| **Materials** | Large whiteboard, coloured markers, fleeces, mats, large drum(s), personal folders and workbooks, crayons and coloured pens. |

Warm Up Invite everyone into the circle and encourage feedback. Introduce the idea that nature is a reality, but that nature can also help us to express feelings about ourselves and others; invite ideas and write them on the board. WGC/ICh.

Activities   It is important to reassure group members that they are not going to be made to look silly by pretending to be a tree, this is an exercise of the imagination.

- ✪ Invite group members to close their eyes and think generally about trees of all different sorts.
- ✪ If they were a tree, what type of tree would it be? Would it have blossoms, leaves, needles? How old is the tree? Where might it be growing?
- ✪ Open your eyes and draw the tree on A4 paper, as large as possible, include all the ideas they have thought about.
- ✪ Colour in as much of the tree as possible.
- ✪ Show in pictures where this tree grows.

| **Sharing** | In pairs, share and discuss the tree pictures. |

| **Closure** | Write one sentence that describes the tree in workbooks; relax with fleeces. |

99 The Forest of the Group (1)

☑ Children ☑ Teenagers

Aims To encourage group members to make connections between the images they have made and their personal development.

Materials Large whiteboard, coloured markers, fleeces, mats, large drum(s), personal folders and workbooks, crayons and coloured pens; tree pictures from previous session.

Warm Up Invite everyone into the circle and encourage feedback from previous session. Discuss ideas about nature, trees and personal experiences, and write the ideas on the board. WGC/ICh.

Activities Invite the group to continue exploring the tree pictures:

- ✪ Place all the drawings on the floor.
- ✪ The group walks around all the pictures, noting any common elements.
- ✪ Introduce the idea of the 'forest of the group'.
- ✪ Everyone can move their picture, placing it where they feel it belongs in the forest: on its own, perhaps linked to others by being near water, near similar trees, and so on.
- ✪ Invite everyone to note the groupings and sub-grouping of the trees.

Sharing Discuss groupings of trees in the forest, and whether they reflect the dynamics of the group or class.

Closure Draw the landscape where your tree grows; relax with fleeces.

The Great Outdoors: Contact with Nature

100 The Forest of the Group (2)

 Children  Teenagers

Aims To acknowledge relationships within the group and personal insights.

Materials Large whiteboard, coloured markers, fleeces, mats, large drum(s), personal folders and workbooks, crayons and coloured pens; tree pictures from previous session.

Warm Up Invite everyone into the circle and encourage feedback from previous sessions, especially about group relationships. WGC/ICh.

Activities Everyone has their tree picture and is invited to recall the groupings of trees in 'The Forest of the Group (1)'.

⊗ Create sub-groups in the forest (individuals who were perhaps on the periphery can also form a sub-group).

⊗ Share pictures and similarities and differences.

⊗ Create a ritualistic scene using sound, movement and drumming, called 'The Guardians of the Forest'.

⊗ Develop the ideas into words, if appropriate.

⊗ Show the scenes to whole group.

Sharing In the large group, discuss the progression from the pictures to the group drama.

Closure Write a few words about 'The Guardian' scene in workbooks; relax with fleeces.

101 Final Closure

☑ Children ☑ Teenagers

Aims To review the previous sessions, acknowledge successes, and close the group.

Materials Large whiteboard, coloured markers, fleeces, mats, large drum(s), personal folders and workbooks, crayons and coloured pens; artwork from previous sessions, Worksheet 26.

Warm Up Invite everyone into the circle and encourage comments and sharing about the fact that this is the final group. The group chooses its favourite warm-up.

Activities Everyone has all their artwork, folders and workbooks:

- ✪ Invite everyone to look through the work completed throughout the sessions.
- ✪ Each person reads through their own workbook and folders, and writes a closing comment, or draws a picture.
- ✪ Share with a partner what you, individually, have learned on the course.
- ✪ Share comments and achievements with the whole group.
- ✪ Encourage group members to comment positively on each other's progress.
- ✪ Give a copy of Worksheet 26 'Certificate of Achievement', to every individual.

Sharing & Closure A drumming ritual in the whole group, with movement and chants.

The Great Outdoors: Contact with Nature

Resources

Worksheets

Worksheets

Resources

Group Contract & Agreement

We are attending the group on the following dates:

_____

We have not all chosen to be here.

Some of us have been asked to be in this group.

We all agree to abide by the group rules as follows:

1 Everyone listens to what other people are saying without interrupting

2 Everyone agrees to behave in a respectful manner to others

3 Everyone agrees that there is no verbal or physical violence

4 Everyone agrees that equipment is not to be broken

5 _____

6 _____

7 _____

Signature or Thumb Print from all Group Members:

I Feel Trapped

Colour the answers in pictures or in words or both:

✖ I feel trapped in: _____

_____

✖ I feel trapped when: _____

_____

✖ I feel trapped by: _____

_____

Where Do I Feel Hurt?

Where do I feel stressed or where does it hurt?

Colour or write on the picture.

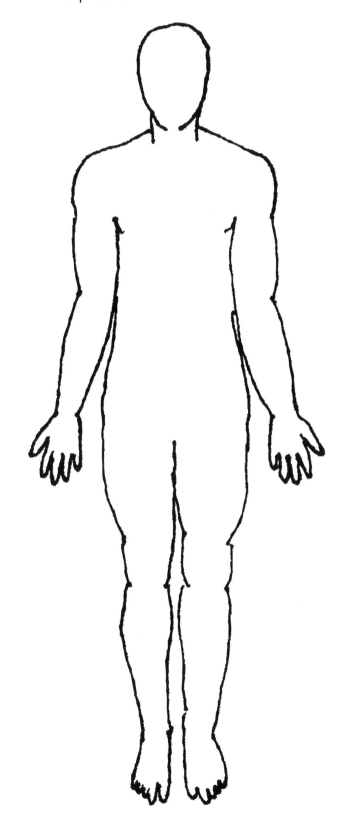

I Feel Lost

Decide where you are on the tree, and colour a leaf person to show where you are.

Colour another leaf person to show where you would like to be.

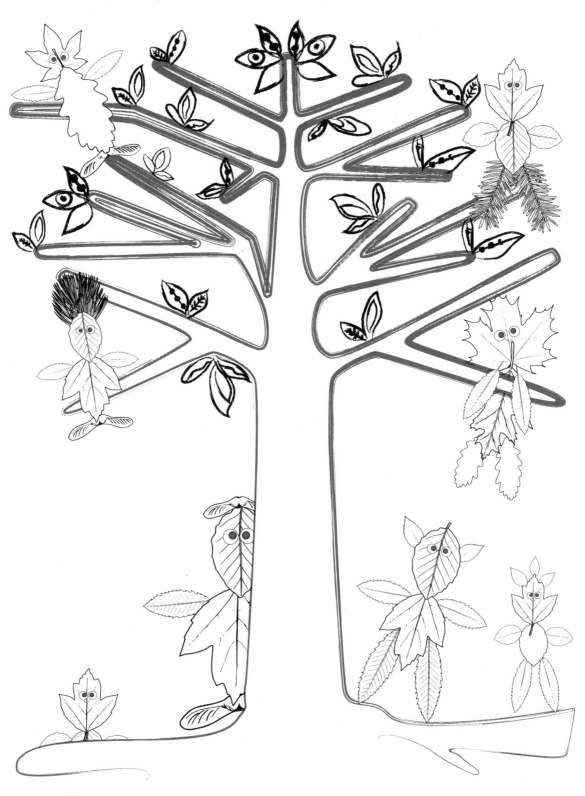

Knitting Myself Back Together

Sometimes people feel 'in bits' or 'unravelled' or 'in holes'

✪ Colour the knitting in positive colours, and fill in the holes

✪ Continue the drawing of the knitting.

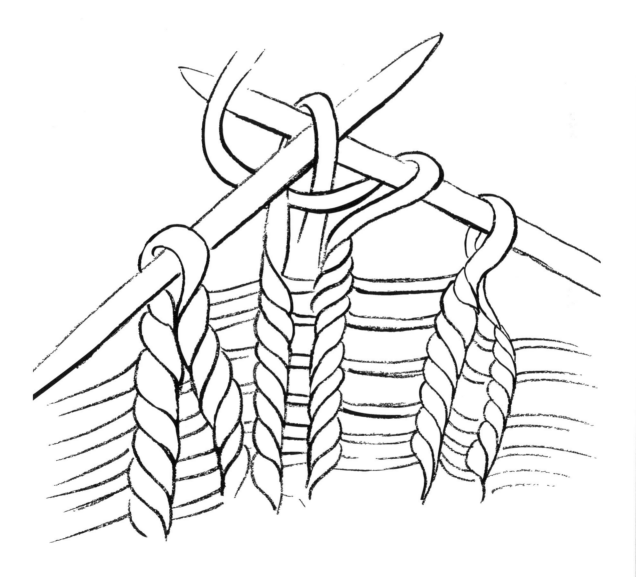

My Rainbow Scarf

Colour the rainbow scarf in colours that make you feel good about yourself.

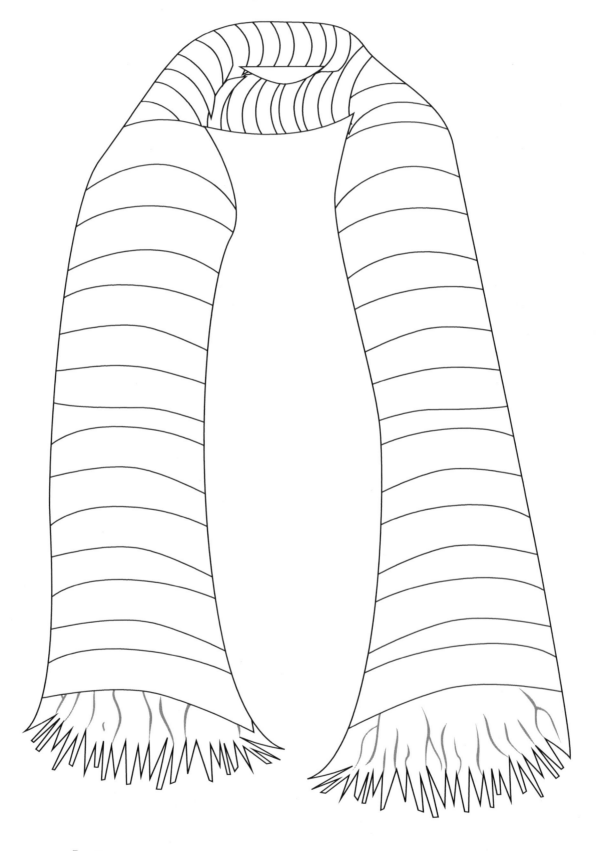

It is Hard to Trust People

Choose which circles to colour.

Draw in the circle the person
or animal you would like to trust

I would like to trust _____

_____

_____

Who Can I Trust? (1)

Choose which circles to draw in:

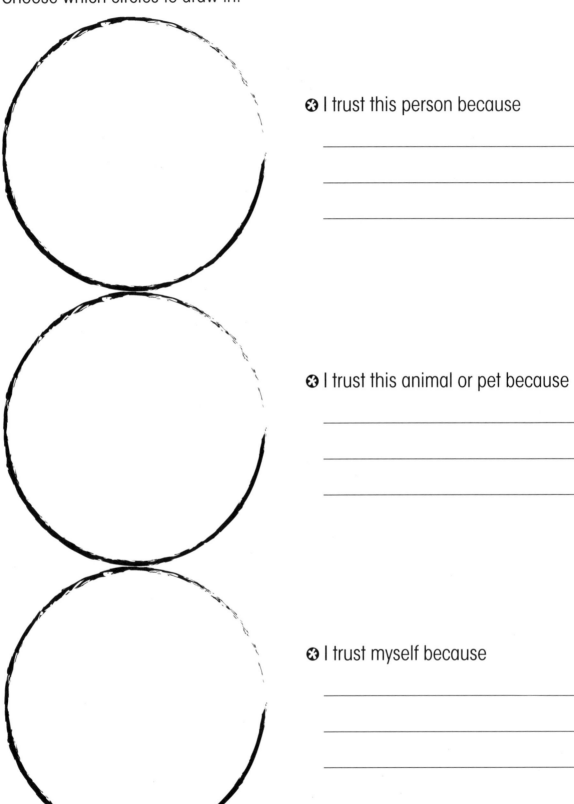

✪ I trust this person because

_____

_____

_____

✪ I trust this animal or pet because

_____

_____

_____

✪ I trust myself because

_____

_____

_____

Who Can I Trust? (2)

Colour the drawing.

I really wish I could trust someone, and they could trust me. If you like, write about the person here: _____

_____

_____

My Tree of Hearts

Colour in a heart for all the special people in your life; you might include:

- ❂ Friends, family, pop-stars, bands, pets, TV people, comic characters....

- ❂ Anyone else who is special to you.

My Tree of Special People

Colour in the tree and write or colour in the circles the people and pets who are special in your life; you might include friends, family, TV people, pets....

Special Words for a Special Friend

Colour in the words that you feel are important ways to describe a friend.

Put your own words in the blank circles.

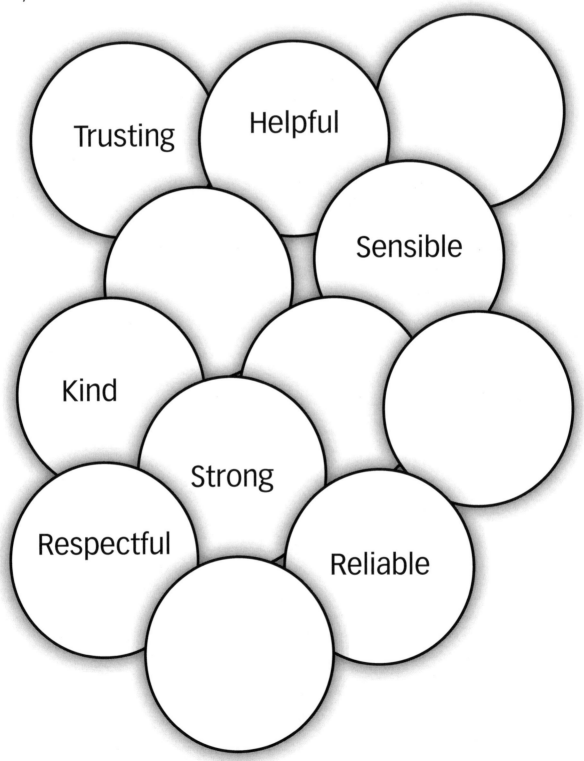

Trusting

Helpful

Sensible

Kind

Strong

Respectful

Reliable

My Special Friend (1)

I have one special friend who I trust, and we have a strong connection.

Colour the knotted rope of your friendship.

My Special Friend (2)

Draw and colour your special friend in the frame and write underneath why this friend is special.

My Special Friend

My Shield of Protection
(that others can see)

When people are scared or bullied they need to think of how to protect themselves. Draw and write on the shield in strong colours, think about words that make you feel strong.

My Shield of Protection
(that only I can see)

Only you can see the inside of the shield. Draw symbols and write positive words that give you strength. You can remember these words to give you confidence.

My Family Tree

Colour in your family members and change any names to suit your own family.

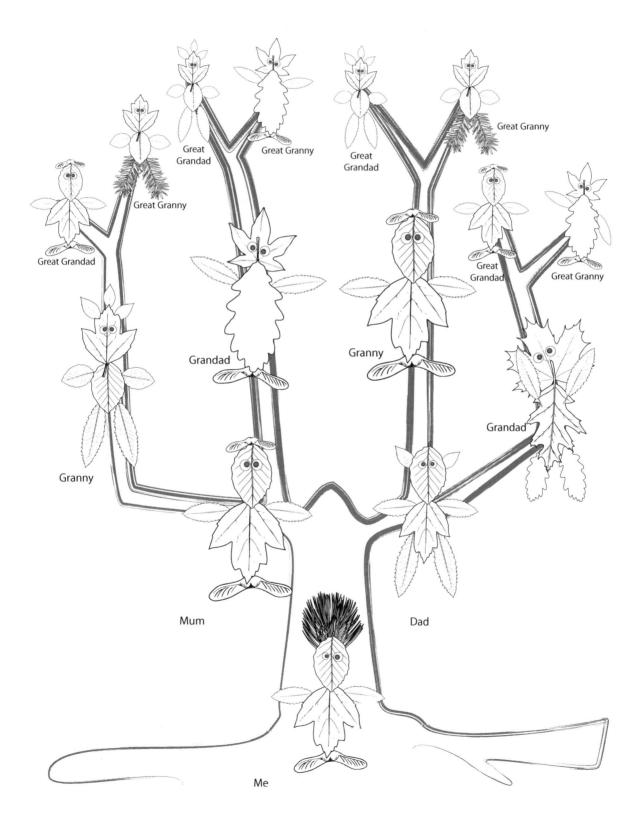

Great Grandad
Great Granny
Great Granny
Great Grandad
Great Granny
Great Grandad
Great Granny
Great Grandad
Great Granny

Grandad
Granny
Granny
Grandad

Mum
Dad

Me

My New Family Tree

Colour in the members of your new family and add new brother(s), new sister(s) and special friends.

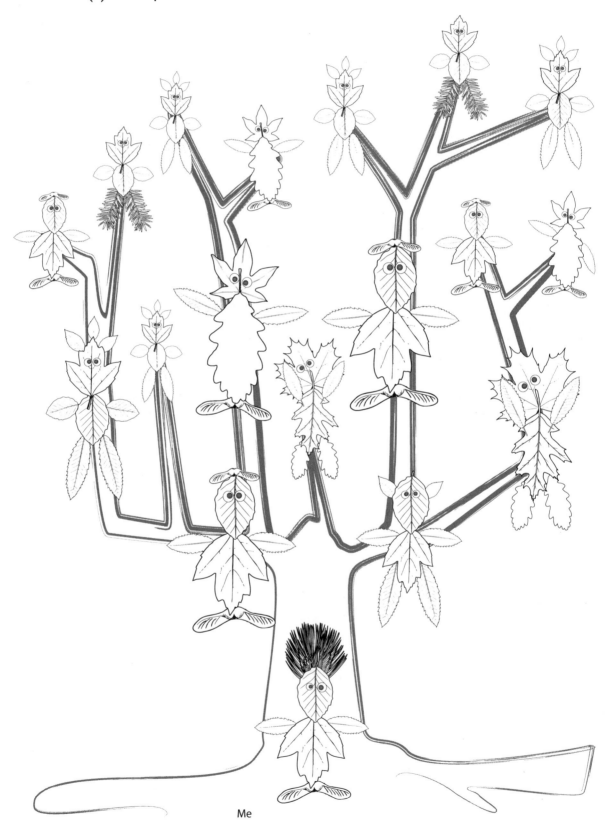

Me

My Dream Family

Colour in and name all the people in your dream family.

Me

I Can Recycle Myself! (1)

This pile of rubbish looks a waste – colour it using bright colours and add some new items to make it look great! Don't forget a frame for your masterpiece!

I Can Recycle Myself! (2)

Colour any words and phrases that you would like to throw in the rubbish bin. On the blank pages write any other words you want to get rid of.

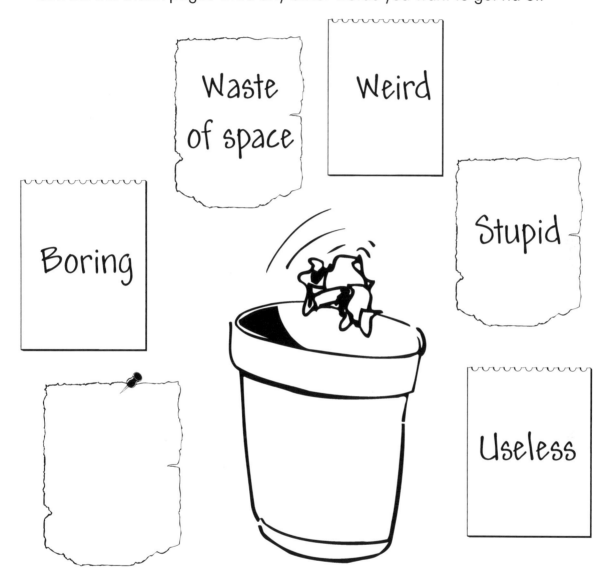

Waste of space

Weird

Boring

Stupid

Useless

Think of the opposites of some of these words and write them in the boxes.

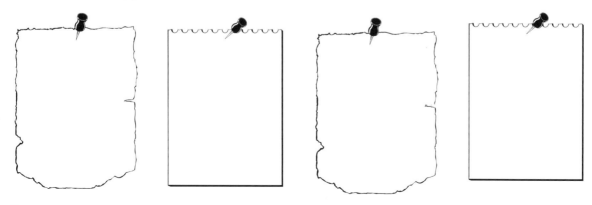

Why Not Let Bygones be Bygones?

Nelson Mandela, after he had been freed from the many years on a harsh prison island, said, 'Let bygones be bygones', and he forgave the people who had treated him so cruelly. He became South Africa's leader, famous for 'reconciliation' rather than 'revenge'.

✪ Colour in the rubbish pile or draw a picture or write the name of anything you can let go of and not want to take revenge over.

✪ Draw a positive image, feeling of symbol.

Choosing the Road

Think about the road you are on at the moment and the things that are not working out. Colour in the old road on the picture.

Think about the positive things that could be on your new road and colour them on the picture.

Take One Step at a Time

Sometimes change feels like a very big step and can be quite scary.

✪ Draw or write in the first small step something you could manage.

✪ Can you take more than one step? Draw and write what your next step might be.

What Would Make a Difference?

Colour in the circles that are important for you, and write new phrases in the blank circles if you wish.

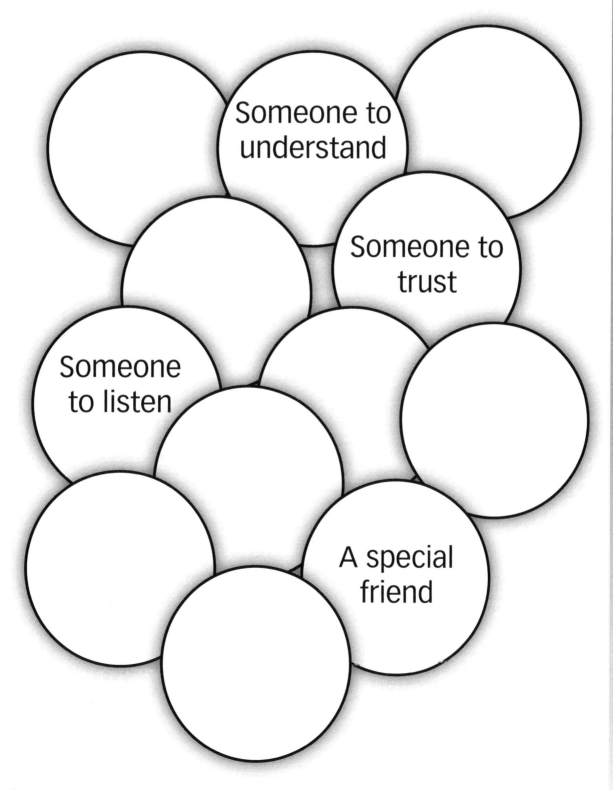

Certificate of Achievement

Certificate of Achievement

Awarded to

_____

has shown skills in the following areas:

_____

_____

and has contributed to the group by:

_____

_____

_____   _____

Signed   Date

The Story of the Worry Tree

This is a story that needs a picture. After you have read the story, perhaps you can draw the Worry Tree and show the bundles that are hanging from the branches. Or draw the bird that flies away with all the worries to a land over the mountains.

When you leave the beautiful garden with the enormous flowers, with peonies as big as cabbages and delphiniums as tall as the hedge, open the little white gate that leads into the meadow. The grass is as tall as your knees, and the grasshoppers are whirring non-stop, and the poppies are bright red in patches like blood. The bright, metallic buttercups shine into chins, and the smells of the wild thyme float on the breeze.

Walking through the meadow towards the woods, it begins to get a little cooler, and there are long shadows from the trees. The first tree is very, very old, with enormous roots and rough bark. Then you see a beautiful golden bird fly down and take some flowers, or perhaps a bundle, from one of the branches and disappear towards the grey mountain. On looking closer, you can see that there are hundreds of little bundles on the tree, hanging by sparkly threads, and a small notice that says, 'You can hang your worries here.'

And, sure enough, the golden bird returns and takes another bundle in its beak, and flies off, over towards the grey mountain.

Ideas

1 Colour the story and decorate it with plants and flowers and insects from the story.

2 Draw the old Worry Tree with its huge roots and rough bark.

3 Think about any worries and draw them, and hang them on the tree

4 Draw and colour the golden bird who carries worries away to the grey mountain.

STORY SHEET 1: ACTIVITY 10

Rock-a-Bye Baby

Rock-a-bye baby,

On the tree top.

When the wind blows,

The cradle will rock.

When the bough breaks,

The cradle will fall.

And down will come baby,

Cradle and all.

Ideas

1 Create a tree around all the words.

2 Draw a cradle in the branches.

3 Draw a safe cradle on the ground with the baby in it.

Helena & Hermia

– O, is all forgot?
All schooldays' friendship, childhood innocence?
We, Hermia, like two artificial gods,
Have with our needles created both one flower,
Both on one sampler, sitting on one cushion,
Both warbling of one song, both in one key,
As if our hands, our sides, voices, and minds
Had been incorporate. So we grew together,
Like to a double cherry – seeming parted,
But yet an union in partition –
Two lovely berries, moulded on one stem;
So, with two seeming bodies but one heart,
Two of the first, like coats in heraldry,
Due but to one and crownèd with one crest.
And will you rent our ancient love asunder
To join with men in scorning your poor friend?
It is not friendly, 'tis not maidenly.
Our sex, as well as I, may chide you for it,
Though I alone do feel the injury.

William Shakespeare, *A Midsummer Night's Dream*
(Act 3, Scene ii)

This is a poem about the friendship between two girls called Helena and Hermia. Helena thinks that Hermia has betrayed her and ganged up with her boyfriend to tease Helena. Think about the words that Helena uses to describe their friendship. How is she feeling about Hermia betraying her?

Colour the poem and decorate it with friendship signs. Think about how you might write a poem about friendship; what words would be important?

The Quarrel

I quarreled with my brother,
I don't know what about,
One thing led to another
And somehow we fell out.
The start of it was slight,
The end of it was strong,
He said he was right,
I knew he was wrong!
We hated one another,
The afternoon turned black.
Then suddenly my brother
Thumped me on the back,
And said, "Oh, come on!
We can't go on all night –
I was in the wrong."
So he was in the right.

Eleanor Farjeon

Ideas

1 Think about how this poem shows very simply how a quarrel starts.

2 Is it typical for brothers and sisters to fall out?

3 Is it hard to give way in an argument?

4 Try writing a poem about a conflict between friends.

5 Draw a picture to illustrate the poem.

The Hunchback in the Park

The hunchback in the park
A solitary mister
Propped between trees and water
From the opening of the garden lock
That lets the trees and water enter
Until the Sunday sombre bell at dark

Eating bread from a newspaper
Drinking water from the chained cup
That the children filled with gravel
In the fountain basin where I sailed my ship
Slept at night in a dog kennel
But nobody chained him up

Like the park birds he came early
Like the water he sat down
And Mister they called Hey Mister
The truant boys from the town
Running when he had heard them clearly
On out of sound

Dylan Thomas (first three verses)

Ideas

1 Read or listen to the verses and be aware of the rhythm of the words.
2 Picture the people and the actions in your mind.
3 Create a picture of how you see the poem.
4 In small groups, make a freeze-frame for each of the verses.

Grandmas

A grandmother is a woman who has no children of her own, and therefore she loves the boys and girls of other people. Grandmothers have nothing to do. They have only got to be there. If they take us for a walk, they go slowly past leaves and caterpillars. They never say, 'Come along quickly', or 'Hurry up for goodness sake!' They are usually fat, but not too fat to tie up our shoe strings. They wear spectacles and sometimes they can take out their teeth. They can answer every question, for instance why dogs hate cats, and why God is not married.

When they read to us they do not leave out anything, and they do not mind if it is always the same story. Everyone should try to have a grandmother, especially those who have no television. Grandmothers are the only grown-ups who always have time.

Written by an eight-year-old boy.

Ideas

1 Draw a picture of the grandma described in the story, and decide what colours she wears.
2 Think about other grandmas, and whether they are very different from this one.
3 Write down what is special about grandmas for you.

The Four Friends

Ernest was an elephant, a great big fellow,
    Leonard was a lion with a six-foot tail,
George was a goat, and his beard was yellow,
    And James was a very small snail.

Leonard had a stall, and a great big strong one,
    Ernest had a manger, and its walls were thick,
George found a pen, but I think it was the wrong one,
    And James sat down on a brick.

A.A. Milne, *When We Were Very Young*

Ideas

1 Which of these four animals do you like the best? Draw a picture of it.

2 Think about how different the four animals are, yet they are still friends. Write or draw about two friends who are very different.

3 Write another verse for this poem that describes the four animals in more detail.

STORY SHEET 7: ACTIVITY 70

References

Cyrulnik B. 2005, *The Whispering of Ghosts: Trauma and Resilience*, Other Press, New York.

Erikson E. 1965/1995, *Childhood and Society*, Vintage, London.

Garbarino J., Dubrow N., Kostelny K. & Pardo C. 1992, *Children in Danger: Coping with the effects of community violence*, Jossey-Bass, CA.

Garmezy N. & Rutter M. (eds) 1983, *Stress, Coping and Development in Children*, McGraw Hill, New York.

Grenville-Cleave B. 2012, *Positive Psychology*, Icon Books, London.

Jennings S. 2011, *Neuro-Dramatic-Play and Attachment*, Jessica Kingsley Publishers, London.

Maston A.E. 2001, 'Ordinary Magic: Resilience processes in development', *American Psychologist*, 56 pp.227–239.

McCarthy D. 2007, *If You Turned into a Monster*, Jessica Kingsley Publishers, London.

Rutter M. 1979, 'Protective Factors in Children's Stress and Disadvantage', in Kent M.W. & Rolf J.E. (eds) *Primary Prevention of Psychopathology, Social Competence in Children*, Vol. 3, University Press of New England, Hanover NH.

Werner E.E. 1990, 'Protective Factors in Individual Resilience', in Meisels S.J. & Shonkoff J.J. (eds) *Handbook of Early Childhood Intervention*, Cambridge University Press, Cambridge.

Williams M. & Penman D. 2011, *Mindfulness: A practical guide to finding peace in a frantic world*, Piatkus, London.

Further Reading

Berger R. & Lahad M. 2013, *The Healing Forest in Post-Crisis Work with Children*, Jessica Kingsley Publishers, London.

Clifford S. & Herrmann A. 1999, *Making a Leap: Theatre of Empowerment*, Jessica Kingsley Publishers, London.

Drost, J. 2011, *Promoting Friendship, Emotional & Social Skills in Children: The Giant's Desk*, Hinton House Publishers, Buckingham.

Gerhardt S. 2004, *Why Love Matters: How Affection Shapes a Baby's Brain*, Brunner-Routledge, Hove.

Jennings S. 2011, *101 Activities for Empathy and Awareness*, Hinton House Publishers, Buckingham.

Jennings S. 2011, *The Anger Management Toolkit*, Hinton House Publishers, Buckingham.

Jennings S. 2013, *Creative Activities for Developing Emotional Intelligence*, Hinton House Publishers, Buckingham.

Lahad M., Shacham M. & Ayalon O. 2013, *The 'BASIC Ph' Model of Coping and Resiliency*, Jessica Kingsley Publishers, London.

Miller A. 1997, *Breaking Down the Wall of Silence to Join the Waiting Child*, Virago, London.

Pearce C. 2011, *A Short Introduction to Promoting Resilience in Children*, Jessica Kingsley Publishers, London.

Resources

101 Activities & Ideas

★ Creative and practical solutions to issues around emotional well-being in young people. Many teachers, care workers and therapists are challenged by difficult behaviours, and families often feel lost for solutions to sudden outbursts or young people's feelings of alienation and lack of self-esteem.

★ Containing a host of ideas for home, school and youth groups, the books will help to tackle these difficult issues in a positive and active way. There are no magic answers, but the ideas aim to empower young people to find solutions to some of their own difficulties, while providing guidance for more positive directions.

★ The books adopt a 'hands-on' approach with a firm and enabling attitude and provide a sound practical basis for active intervention for behaviour change.

101 Activities for Empathy & Awareness
ISBN: 978-1-906531-33-1

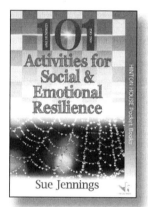

101 Activities for Social & Emotional Resilience
ISBN: 978-1-906531-46-1

101 Ideas for Managing Challenging Behaviour
ISBN: 978-1-906531-44-7

101 Activities for Increasing Focus & Motivation
ISBN: 978-1-906531-45-4

101 Activities for Positive Thoughts & Feelings
ISBN: 978-1-906531-47-8

www.hintonpublishers.com

The Stories Within

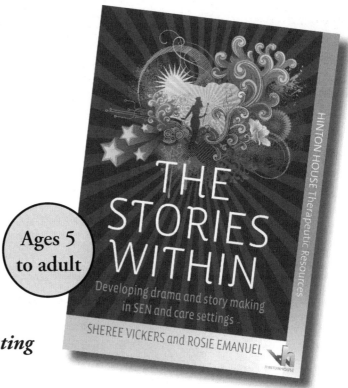

Developing inclusive drama and story-making

Sheree Vickers & Rosie Emanuel

A comprehensive toolkit for creating inclusive drama & storytelling.

This practical, photocopiable book provides an innovative approach to developing inclusive story-making and drama with both children and adults.

Emphasises developing original stories rather than using traditional storylines or scripts, shows how to create drama games or adapt existing ones to the specific needs of your group.

Includes: Preparation & planning; Creating a sensory storytelling kit; Developing inclusive practice in schools and groups; Working with adults: rediscovering play & creating age-appropriate stories; Practical workshop structures; Problems, strategies & solutions.

Ideal for use by teachers, drama practitioners and therapists this practical handbook provides the tools needed to create original drama and stories. These ideas can be used with individuals and groups with a variety of needs.

ISBN 978-1-906531-22-5

www.hintonpublishers.com